Texas

Indian

Troubles

By Hilory G. Bedford

Edited by Michelle M. Haas

Copano Bay Press
2011

Originally pubished in 1905 by the author under the same title.

Copano Bay Press Edition
Copyright 2011

ISBN 978-0-9829828-8-4

Contents

Publisher's Note, 9
Introductory, 11
Author's Preface, 13
Dedicatory, 17

EARLY SETTLERS & THE INDIANS, 19

PAST, PRESENT & FUTURE OF AMERICAN INDIANS, 23

THE SCALPING OF JOSIAH WILBARGER, 27

KILLING OF THE GOACHER FAMILY
& CAPTURE OF MRS. CRAWFORD - 1840, 35

CAPTURE & ESCAPE OF MRS. WEBSTER, 39

COUNCIL HOUSE FIGHT AT SAN ANTONIO, 43

SACKING OF LINNVILLE, 47

BATTLE OF PLUM CREEK - AUGUST 1840, 50

THE RAID ON PARKER'S FORT, 56

THE CAPTIVES OF PARKER'S FORT, 60

CYNTHIA ANN PARKER, 64

BATTLES ON THE CANADIAN RIVER, 67

BATTLE OF THE WICHITA MOUNTAINS, 70

BATTLE OF PEASE RIVER
& RECAPTURE OF CYNTHIA ANN PARKER, 73

ELDRIDGE PEACE COMMISSION, 81

TREATMENT OF THE INDIANS BY THE U.S. GOVERNMENT, 87

MURDER OF THE BABB FAMILY, 93

ELM CREEK RAID OF 1864, 96

NEGRO BRIT'S FAMILY, 100

BIG FOOT WALLACE, 104

WALLACE'S MAVERICK, 118

BIG FOOT WALLACE & THE INDIAN HATER, 121

ANECDOTE OF TOM BIRD, 131

SCHOOLHOUSE MASSACRE, 133

SALT CREEK MASSACRE, 139

DILLARD BROTHERS' FIGHT WITH THE INDIANS, 153

KILLING & SCALPING OF NICK DAWSON, 155

MASSACRE OF CAMERONS AND MASONS, 159

FATHER TACKETT'S INDIAN FIGHT, 162

CAPTURE & ESCAPE OF MRS. SHEGOG, 167

MURDER OF THE HUFF FAMILY, 170

KILLING OF KEENON'S & PASCHAL'S FAMILIES, 173

YANKEE WHO WANTED TO KILL AN INDIAN, 181

RIGGS KILLED, LITTLE GIRLS ESCAPED, 184

OUTRAGES IN UVALDE COUNTY, 188

"HOG-MY-CATS" BOWLES, 191

THE WHIPPING OF HENRY SHANE, 192

MRS. ROBINSON DEFENDS HER CHILDREN, 193

MRS. KINCHELOE BADLY WOUNDED, 195

JUDGE MARTIN & HIS SERVANT KILLED, 197

CAPTURE OF THE BALL BOYS, 200

CAPTAIN EARHEART KILLS A RED-HEADED INDIAN, 202

CAPTAIN STEPHENS & HIS MEN SURROUNDED, 204

LAST INDIAN RAID IN JACK & WISE COUNTIES, 206

OLIVER LOVING KILLED ON THE PECOS, 210

THE THRILLING HISTORY OF THE FRIENDS, 212

WHY I NEVER FOUGHT THE INDIANS, 220

THE INDIANS' FOOD SUPPLY FOR RAIDS, 227

Publisher's Note

To the memory of my grandparents, Nanny and Papa, this rare and little known tome about pioneer life among the Texas Indians is dedicated. We are the children of children, and we live as we are shown.

-*Michelle M. Haas, Managing Editor*
Windy Hill

INTRODUCTORY

The author has been a resident of Texas since 1850 and in constant touch, during that time, with frontier life and, to some extent, an interested observer of the different stages of progress made by civilization in claiming for posterity this great southwestern territory. On account of his own personal knowledge and experience of many of its thrilling scenes and his intimate acquaintance with other frontiersmen who have, in various parts of the border, encountered the hardships, privations and dangers of frontier life, his interest in the welfare and progress of civilization along the border has been kept constantly aglow.

Many of his friends have insisted upon his giving to the public, as his contribution to the unwritten history of his adopted State, some of the incidents which have been gathered during his half century upon the border. That the story of his own personal experiences may be more fully understood and appreciated, he finds it necessary to recount some of the facts and review their results, preceding his advent into Texas, so that the reader may the better understand the environments that abounded at the time he became identified with this history of the country. Some of these facts may be obtained from published histories, and others have been obtained by the author from actual participants with whom he was acquainted, and it is hoped that these additional facts not previously recorded will add some interest to these pages.

AUTHOR'S PREFACE

In the history of Indian troubles in Texas, we are made to look upon the serious side of life, as it brings to mind the friends and things of long ago.

Many scenes depicted in this book touch the deepest sympathies of our hearts, not alone because our own personal friends were participants in them, but because of the thrilling nature of the things related.

The main object of this book will be to place on record a correct history of the facts connected with, and the sacrifices made by, the early settlers in order to redeem this great land from the hands of the roving bands of Indians that had always occupied it and had done nothing to improve or develop it.

Brave generals have led strong armies on to victory, and their friends have had these generals' lives written in the histories of their country, and often these men were cruel, hard-hearted men, forging their way to place and power by brutal force. Hero worship is wrong, but to honor the noble patriots of our country is right. They ought to be held in affectionate and grateful remembrance. That is the strength of a free country. It is the bulwark of American liberty.

We have erected monuments to the memories of Washington, Jackson and many others, whose deeds of valor and patriotic service well deserve it. This is right. While it is but just to the dead, it is also a benefit to the living, for in this way the rising generations are inspired to follow their noble examples. And whatever gives noble impulses and lofty aspirations to the young benefits the country in a permanent way.

Texas has a history that is peculiar. There is a line of patriots in Texas history whose names outshine that of any other country. Austin, Ross, Bowie, Travis, Milam and Houston were some of the grandest men that ever graced the earth. At a cattlemen's convention in St. Louis, an old man told me he had been asked why Texas was called the Lone Star State, but that he could not answer it. This ought not to be the case with any old Texan. The reason why Texas is called the Lone Star State ought to be known to every Texas citizen. They need only look back to the storming of the Alamo and the brutal murder of the Mier prisoners and those at Goliad. All the while, Mexican soldiers have been present across our Southwestern frontier, while at the same time roving bands of savage Indians were plundering our settlements, murdering our people, and carrying away innocent women and children as captives. And when the war clouds seemed the darkest, General Houston, with his little army of Texas patriots, pounced upon Santa Anna's overwhelming forces, capturing their commanding General and his army, and thus secured the independence of the Republic of Texas, and unfurled to the breezes our flag, bearing the single star.

As Texas had secured her independence by her own patriotism and chivalry, she became the owner of her public domain of land, and still retains it since she has been attached to the United States. From her public lands, Texas has acquired the most magnificent school funds of any of the great compact of the States, and still holds proud preeminence over all her sister States. This great country hasn't fallen into our hands by accident, nor has it been purchased for a trifle.

For over fifty years, our people pushed forward, step by step, driving back the Indians and settling and developing the country. How often this required sacrifice, hardship and danger. Many have fallen and now sleep in unmarked graves, and how many have fallen and their bones left to bleach, unburied, among the hills and valleys of a wild, unsettled country.

The question may be asked, why did they not give back an inch when they saw they were in great danger? In the first place, to give back at all was equal to surrendering the whole land, for each mile that the whites would retreat, the Indians would at once claim ten more. To give back meant to surrender home with all that home meant. The love of home forbade it; patriotism forbade it; heroic manhood forbade it. And, sustained by these principles, the early settlers faced danger unmoved, and their noble, unselfish lives should ever be held in grateful remembrance.

It has been suggested that we have an annual reunion, that we may come together to enjoy each other's society and talk over times gone by. There, we may bring to remembrance many of the trials and sufferings borne by those that stood side by side with us during those dark and trying times, but who have long since passed to their reward and, we trust, to where they will hear the Indian war-whoop no more. Nor will the shrieks and groans of those who are being scalped and murdered ever pierce their ears again, nor their peaceful repose ever be disturbed by the wail of innocent women and children that are being dragged from their homes as captives by cruel, merciless foes. We want to come together to recount the deeds of valor done by them, and renew the ties of friendship and love that they may ever be held in grateful remembrance by our children and our children's children.

The rising generation, as well as the teeming thousands that have immigrated to this country, ought to know something of the cost of the blessings that we now enjoy. We bid a hearty welcome to all good people, and ask them to join us in honoring and remembering those by whose grace we are enabled to enjoy this pleasant, peaceful land. We cannot place a marble shaft at the head of each grave, but we can record in a book a correct and authentic account of what our frontier people did have to undergo. We cannot afford to leave things so sacred to memory alone, for time changes all things, and soon these matters would all go into the forgotten past. Instead we will commit them to record in a book, and hand it down to the coming generations. This book will not only perpetuate the fondest memories of the friends of the past, but there is also to be found a source of interest and pleasure in these thrilling scenes that give a spice to life that it would not otherwise have without them.

DEDICATORY

To the sacred memory of those who, during the dark and trying times when the savage and merciless Indians were plundering and pillaging our country, scalping and killing innocent women and children, and carrying away many into a captivity worse than death, braved the dangers and bore the sufferings and hardships of a Texas frontier; to those who sacrificed their lives, and now sleep in their unknown and unmarked graves; to those who fell victims to the savage foe far away among the hills and valleys of a wild and unsettled country, their bones left to bleach unburied where they fell; this work is affectionately and respectfully dedicated by the author.

I have not been able to record the names of each, but have endeavored to present a correct account of their lives, their sufferings and heroic conduct, so that the rising generations may be reminded of the fact that this magnificent country has not fallen into their possession by accident, nor has it been purchased for a trifle. It was won with the blood and tears, sorrows and sufferings of noble patriots who, for so many years, braved perils and faced a savage foe whose religion seemed to be to kill and torture our people as they stood in defense of their country and their homes.

We owe them a debt of gratitude, for had they shrank from their duty in the least, the Indians would have taken every advantage, and this country would have long remained a wild and unsettled wilderness. The thousands of happy, prosperous people who are now occupying peaceful homes where none dare molest or make afraid, would never have been induced to loose their moorings in another country and settle in our fair land, nor would we have all the many things that make for the good of man and the glory of God. The roving bands of hostile Indians have been brought into subjection. The wilderness has been converted into a blooming garden, and the solitary place has been made to resound with the songs of hope and joy by a peaceful, happy people.

Peace and honor to those who fell in the awful struggle, and all honor to the few battle-scarred veterans who survived the mighty conflict and, although bending under the weight of years, are permitted to spend their declining days in peace, happiness and prosperity in a country that flows with milk and honey, and blossoms like a rose.

HILORY G. BEDFORD

EARLY SETTLERS AND THE INDIANS

The early settlers of Texas were a bold, hardy people and, coming into a wild, unsettled country, they were naturally expected to have to undergo hardships and privations. Not only this, but they expected to face the dangers incident to frontier life. These dangers were not only from the red men that occupied the wild country, but from wild beasts that roamed at will through the forests and over the plains.

While this was the case, the fine fish and game furnished a very luxurious meat supply. This, with the wild honey from the bee trees in the forests, gave all of their food as a gift from natural fields. And thus we see that the incentives that led them out to the front also prepared them for any emergency that might arise. Good firearms were the first things thought of in their equipment. Bread was the only article of food that required any effort to obtain. It was scarce and hard to get and, therefore, was used very economically and was often supplemented with dried meats.

Clothing, to a great extent, was obtained from the same source, as the settlers were so remote from the markets. Therefore, the hides of the wild animals were used for this purpose and, while they did not make very tasteful garments, they were a necessity and were very comfortable as well as very durable.

All these things were a means of adapting the whole people—men, women and children—to the frontier life for, in this way, all were interested in watching for the wild game, and the excitements of the chase were enjoyed by all alike. Thus they formed the habits suited to the frontier life and were, in some respects, like the Indians, except that the settlers opened for themselves farms and began the pursuit of agriculture. They prepared homes and arranged for domestic life.

Around their homes, the bounding deer and antelope could be seen, and wild turkeys and smaller game of different kinds could be seen almost any time. But the wild horses (mustangs) would come in view occasionally and, in the proper season, the fine, fat bear and the buffalo were secured without any great effort. I have often thought that one of the most enjoyable scenes I ever witnessed was a frontier cabin, or camp, with a good assortment of game strung up around it, for every member of the family enjoyed this, even the women and the little ones. And when the country would begin to settle up so as to drive out the game, the whole family was ready to move on west, to find a new range where the game was more plentiful.

When making a talk before an audience in which there were several of those old frontiersmen, when I began to describe for them some of the scenes I had enjoyed in the early days, I remarked that if there was another frontier to which we could go, I believed that these old-timers would all go to it at once. In their excitement, several of them sprang to their feet, exclaiming, "Yes sir! We would be off for it tomorrow!"

While the early settlers were a rugged people, and may have lacked something in the way of culture and refinement, they were a noble people. Their hospitality and proverbial honesty, as well as their courage and patriotism, were their most worthy characteristics. When they came to this new country and found it occupied, to some extent, by the Indians, they treated them kindly and showed them the same kindness that they showed each other. The Indians were very kind to their friends and always ready to show this kindness in a practical way, but the Indians had other peculiarities that should be known to properly understand them. Once aroused, they were revengeful enemies. It was a part of their religion to kill for revenge. When bad white men—renegades and fugitives from justice back in the States, many of them murderers and thieves that could not live in civil society—got in with the wild Indians whose natural disposition as well as their lifelong training was to be expert thieves and to kill for revenge, the Indians were really made worse.

It must be said that these Indians had been in continual war from time immemorial among themselves, and they had no fixed dwelling place. They had no rules for adjusting their differences between the different tribes and, in reality, their lives were but little better than the wild beasts upon which they fed. Though it may be said that they were incited to their deeds of barbarity by bad white men, they were very susceptible to being thus influenced.

The idea that the white people have taken the red man's country is a gross error, for the Indians only occupied this country as the wild beasts did, and they have never done anything to establish their rights to this country. "The earth is the Lord's and the fullness thereof. God made man and set him over the works of his hands." He was to go out into the earth and subdue it. He was to make his living by the sweat of his brow. Every man has a right to so much of this world as he can use for the glory of God and the good of mankind. The Indians have never met any of the responsibilities placed upon them by their Creator.

When we look at Texas as it was, and then look at it as it is today, by watching the march of progress as this great State is being developed, we are forced to conclude that the Lord is blessing the works of the white man, and that this is the white man's country. It is now opened to the world by the efforts of the white man, and is thus to be made prosperous country for the millions to make their homes in. While those who first settled here do not wish to hold any exclusive claims over the country, we do ask everyone to consider what has been done to redeem this great land from a wild wilderness infested with wild beasts and savage Indians, and that this wilderness has been made to blossom like a garden. Although this country is now so peaceful and so prosperous, if we follow the history of Texas Indian troubles as given in the following chapters of this book, we will see that the early history of Texas is written along lines that have been traced with the tears of weeping mothers, fathers, sisters and brothers. We see the dark forms of our savage foes as they recede from our civilization. We see their cruel hands dripping with the blood of the best people of our country, and we hear the plaintive cries of innocent captives in their merciless hands.

Past, Present & Future of American Indians

The American Indians have been a subject of study to our people for a long time. Their past condition is well known and, as I have brought out some of their native peculiarities in another chapter, I will not enter into their past history so thoroughly, but will look into their present condition and then anticipate their final destiny as best I can.

It is needless to try to account for their being on the American continent, or for their origin, further than to simply say that they, as well as all mankind, spring from the same parentage. There are so many theories advanced as to their origin that we cannot adopt any of them further than to present some of the most plausible lines of reasoning that are followed by those who have had the best opportunities to inform themselves in regard to the matter.

Bancroft, in his history of them, says that they, as well as the negroes, have at least one strong bit of evidence that they sprang from the same parentage that the Anglo-Saxon, or white people, did—their amalgamation only increases their power of reproduction. It is a law in all animated nature that where two distinct lines of animals are crossed, they lose their power of reproduction. For instance, the ass and the horse lose their power of reproduction in the mule. Bancroft also says that different kinds of wolves interbreeding bring about the same result. But when the darker species of mankind are crossed with the whites, it only makes them more prolific, and this is readily apparent among the mulattoes of the South.

Let the question of the origin of the Indians be settled as it may. They were in this country when it was first discovered, and had never done anything towards its development. Their conditions, in most respects, were not so good as they are now, for the Indians then lived in continual warfare with each other, which now they are not allowed to do. Especially is this warfare prohibited between the different tribes, and when they kill each other at all, they are held accountable to the law, and life and property are protected for them just as it is for the whites. While their tribal distinctions are still observed and their own regulations permitted, they now have all the protection to life, liberty and property that law and equity will give them under their peculiar circumstances.

In setting apart to them their lands for their homes, the very best of the best country obtainable was allotted to them, and this has not occurred accidentally. They were allowed to choose their places as tribes and then, when they took the land as individuals, they showed good judgment in getting the richest valleys and best watered places along streams. The United States government is further protecting the Indians from shrewd white men in not allowing them to part with their homes for a period of time sufficient for them to know the value of property, and for them to realize how important it is to have homes and become located instead of leading the wild, rambling life they had always lived. Not only is the magnanimity of the Indian's white friends shown in giving them homes and protecting them from their own murderous practices, but they are being taught the great principles that underlie a happy, peaceful life. But for this, they could never aspire to such a high degree of culture.

Now, since they are furnished with splendid school buildings of their own and of which they are justly proud, where their children are given good literary, as well as moral instruction, and their present condition is so superior to their former state, it certainly can never be said that the white man is an intruder and trespasser on the Indian's rights in this country. They are also clothed, fed and, to some extent, housed until they learn how to adapt themselves to domestic life and to acquire their own living from agricultural pursuits.

It is with some degree of hesitancy and caution that we venture to anticipate their future destiny as a people. It seems to me that this great question will ultimately be settled upon the great principle of the "survival of the fittest." However, I think that it is seldom that this principle prevails anywhere. But since we see them so incapable of refined social enjoyment and so slow to take hold of and improve the opportunities afforded them, we can't but conclude that they will someday pass away as a people. The white people are giving them all the advantages of their progress in science and internal developments, yet the Indians are on the decline, and the inferior are slowly receding before the superior.

Gen. Porter, a Cherokee Indian, put this thing before one of our National Cattlemen's Conventions at St. Louis, in the prettiest way of anyone I've ever heard on the subject. It was at a time when all the stockmen of the whole country were organizing for the purpose of mutual protection, and each part of the country was represented by delegates selected by the stockmen of the country. Gen. Porter was making a plea for the people of the Indian Territory, that they might have proper representation in the association.

He said that "when the Indians were in full and undisturbed possession of the range country, they were like the sun at mid-day, when it is shining in all of its beauty and strength; it then passes over to where it goes slowly down the Western sky until it passes behind the lofty peaks of the Rocky Mountains, and throws back its last rays of light over their then towering summits like streams of gold, which gradually fade away until it grows dark, and we say the sun has gone down. But we know it will rise again to gladden and brighten another day."

Then he turned, as if to shift the scene, and with his voice trembling with emotion, he said, "Not so with us! Not so with us! Our sun has gone down. It will rise no more. Then others will occupy our homes, and other hands will handle our things, and we will pass away to be forgotten. But while we are here we ask it, and I believe we will receive what we ask, and that is that we have but equal rights with others."

THE SCALPING OF JOSIAH WILBARGER

Of this tragic event I have no personal knowledge whatso-
ever, never having met any of the participants mentioned,
but I give it as found in Wilbarger's *Indian Depredations
in Texas*. It tells of some strange premonitions that came
to some of the participants coincident with the incidents
themselves, making for a remarkably strange story. It
would be far more difficult for me to believe the statements
as given in the account had I not once had a presentiment
equally as strange as the one here stated.

I do not give this account because it borders on the
miraculous, but because it gives a correct account of the
dreadful troubles through which those people passed.
They endured it for the purpose of winning this fine country from the possession of blood-thirsty fiends in human
form, whose principle occupation was murder and who,
when not inflicting it upon the whites, were engaged in
equally as cruel murders among themselves or other tribes
of Indians. This beautiful country had remained in their
possession for ages past, with no sign of development and
today, after but a few decades of white settlement, it is
furnishing homes for the multitudes who are making the
wilderness blossom. From Wilbarger's history:

"In the spring of 1830, Stephen F. Austin came to his new
colony located on the upper Colorado, with two survey-
ors and the advance guard of immigrants, for the purpose
of establishing the surveys of those who had made their
selections. Josiah Wilbarger and Reuben Hornsby were
among those who had previously been on the ground and
made their selections for their headright leagues. Wilbarger came to Texas from Missouri as early as 1828, and had
settled in Matagorda County where he remained about
one year, then moved up the Colorado. It was about the
month of March, 1830, that he selected a beautiful valley
ten miles above where the San Antonio and Nacogdoches
Road crosses the river, and where the town of Bastrop now

stands. This was on what is known as Wilbarger's Creek, and was his headright survey. Immediately after making his selection, he moved his family upon his league. He had with him two or three transient young men, and they built his house. His nearest neighbor was about twenty-five miles down the river.

"In the month of April, Austin, with his surveying party accompanied by Reuben Hornsby, Webber Duty and others who had previously made selections, arrived and commenced work on the Colorado River, where the San Antonio and Nacogdoches Road crosses. The river was meandered to the upper corner of the Jessee Tannahill league, where the party quit work in the month of May. Wilbarger was the first and only outside settler in Austin's new colony until July of 1832, when Reuben Hornsby came up from Bastrop, where he had stopped for a year or two, and occupied his league on the east bank of the Colorado River, some nine miles below where the City of Austin now stands.

"Hornsby's house was always noted for hospitality, and he, like his neighbor Wilbarger, was noted for these virtues and that personal courage which marked them both as men among the early settlers. Young men, who from time to time came out upon the frontier as prospectors, made Hornsby's house a stopping place and were always welcomed, for it was chiefly through such visits that news from the States could be obtained. A more beautiful tract, even now, could not be found, than the league of land belonging to Reuben Hornsby. Washed on one side by the Colorado, it stretches over a level valley three miles wide to the east and was, at the time of which we write, covered by wild rye, which give it the appearance of a vast wheat field. Such was this valley in its virgin state that it tempted Hornsby to build and risk his family outside of the settlements. Until a few years ago, not an acre of that land had ever been sold, but was occupied by the children and grandchildren of the old pioneer, who lived out his fourscore years and died without a blemish on his character.

"In August of 1833, a man named Christian and his wife were living with Hornsby, and several young unmarried men were also stopping there. This was customary in those days, and the people were glad to have them around for protection. Two young men, Standifer and Haynie, had just come into the settlement from Missouri to look at the country. Early in August, Josiah Wilbarger came up to Hornsby's and, in company with Christian, Strother, Standifer and Haynie, rode out in a northwestern direction to look at the surrounding country. When riding up Walnut Creek some five or six miles from where the City of Austin stands, they discovered an Indian, but he refused to parley with them upon being hailed by them, and went off in the direction of a mountain covered with cedar to the west of them. They gave chase and pursued him to the mountains near the head of Walnut Creek, near where James Rodgers afterwards settled.

"Returning from the chase, they stopped for noon and refreshed themselves about half a mile up the branch above Pecan Springs, and four miles east of where Austin was afterwards established, in sight of the road now leading from Austin to Manor. Wilbarger, Christian and Strother unsaddled their horses and hoppled them out to graze, but Haynie and Standifer left their horses saddled and staked them. While the men were eating, they were suddenly fired on by Indians. The trees near them were not large and offered poor protection. Each man sprang behind a tree and promptly returned the fire of the savages, who had stolen up afoot under cover of the brush and timber, having left their horses out of sight.

"Wilbarger's party had fired about a couple of rounds when a ball struck Christian, breaking his thigh bone. Strother had already been mortally wounded. Wilbarger sprang to the side of Christian and set him up by the side of his tree. Christian's gun was loaded but not primed. A ball from one of the Indian's guns bursted Christian's powderhorn. Wilbarger primed his gun and then jumped behind his own tree. At this time, Wilbarger received an arrow through the calf of his leg and had received a flesh wound in his hip. Scarcely had Wilbarger gotten behind his tree when he received another arrow through the calf of the other leg.

"Up to this time, Standifer and Haynie had fought right on with the others. But when they saw Strother mortally wounded and Christian disabled, they mounted their horses that were still standing saddled. Wilbarger hailed them and asked them, if they wouldn't stay and fight, to let him get up behind one of them. He ran to overtake them, wounded as he was, for some distance, but was struck with a ball from behind, which penetrated about the center of his neck and came out to the left of his chin. He fell apparently dead but, though unable to speak or move, did not lose consciousness. He was conscious when the Indians came around him, when they stripped him naked and tore the scalp from his head. He says, though paralyzed and unable to move, he knew what was being done, and when his scalp was torn from his head. It created no pain from which he could flinch, but it sounded just like distant thunder.

"The Indians cut the throats of Christian and Standifer, but the character of Wilbarger's wound made them think that his neck was broken, and that he was surely dead. This certainly saved his life. When Wilbarger recovered consciousness, the evening was far spent. He had lost much blood, and it was still slowly ebbing from his wound. He was alone in the wilderness, naked and bleeding. Consumed by an intolerable thirst, he dragged himself to a pool of water, and lay in it for an hour, when he became so chilled and numbed that it was with difficulty he moved to dry land. Being warmed by the sun and being so weak, he fell into a deep sleep. When he awoke, the blood had ceased to flow from his neck, but he was again suffering from thirst and was hungry.

"After crawling back and drinking, he crawled out over the grass, picking up anything to appease his hunger. The green flies had blown his wounds while he was asleep and the maggots had begun to work, which pained him very much and gave him much uneasiness. As night came on, he determined to go as far as he could in the direction of Reuben Hornsby's, about six miles off. He had gone about six hundred yards when he sank down, exhausted, to the ground under a large post oak tree, almost despairing of life. Those who have ever spent a summer night in Austin know that, in that climate, the nights are very cool, and anyone sleeping out in those nights needs some cover. Wilbarger, wounded, naked, suffering and feeble, suffered after midnight intensely with cold. No sound fell upon his ear but the hooting owls and the bar of the lone coyote wolf, while above him the bright, silent starts seemed to mock his agony.

"We will now state two incidents that are so mysterious that they would excite our incredulity, were it not for the high character of those who to their dying day vouched for their truth.

"As Wilbarger lay under the oak tree, prone on the ground, he distinctly saw, standing near him, the spirit of his sister, Margaret Clifton, who had died the day before in Florisant, in St. Louis County, Missouri. She said to him, 'Brother Josiah, you are too weak to go by yourself. Remain where you are, and friends will come to help you before the setting of the sun.' When she said this, she moved in the direction of Hornsby's house. In vain, he besought her to remain with him until help should come.

"Haynie and Standifer on reaching Hornsby's had reported the death of their three companions, stating that they saw Wilbarger fall and about fifty Indians around him, and knew that he was dead. That night, Mrs. Hornsby startled from her sleep and woke her husband. She told him that she confidently believed that Wilbarger was alive; that she had seen him vividly in a dream—naked, wounded and scalped—but she knew he lived. Soon she fell asleep again. Wilbarger again appeared to her—alive, wounded, naked and scalped—so vividly that she woke Mr. Hornsby and told him her dream, saying 'I know Mr. Wilbarger is not dead.' So confident was she that she would not permit the men to sleep longer, but had the coffee and breakfast ready by daylight, and urged the men at the house to start to Wilbarger's relief.

"The relief party consisted of Joseph Rodgers, Reuben Hornsby, Webber, John Walters and others. As they approached the tree under which Wilbarger had passed the night, Rodgers was in advance and saw Wilbarger, who was sitting at the root of the tree. He presented a ghastly appearance, for his body was almost covered with blood. Rodgers, mistaking him for an Indian, yelled, 'Here they are boys!' Then Wilbarger rose up and said, 'Boys, it is Wilbarger; don't shoot.'

"When the relief party started out, Mrs. Hornsby gave her husband three sheets. Two of them were placed over the bodies of Christian and Strother until the next day when the men returned and buried them. The last of the sheets was placed around Wilbarger, who was placed upon Rodgers' horse, and Hornsby, being lighter than the rest, mounted behind him and, with his arms around Wilbarger, sustained him in the saddle. The next day, William Hornsby (who is still living), Joseph Rodgers, Walter and one or two others, returned to bury Christian and Strother.

"When Wilbarger was found, the only particle of clothing left behind by the savages was one sock. He had torn that from his foot, which was very much swollen from an arrow wound in his leg, and had placed it on his naked skull, from which his scalp had been taken. He was tenderly cared for by his friends at Hornsby's house. For some days his scalp was dressed with bear's oil, and when he recovered sufficiently to move, he was placed in a sled by William Hornsby and Leman Barker, his father-in-law, because he could not endure the motion of a wagon, and was thus carried several miles down the river to his own cabin.

"Josiah Wilbarger lived eleven years. The scalp never grew entirely over the bone. A small patch in the middle remained bare, over which he always wore a covering. The bone became diseased and exfoliated, finally exposing the brain. His death was hastened, as Dr. Anderson, his physician, thought, by his striking his head against the low door of his gin-house many years after he was scalped."

Here, Wilbarger's book states, "We have stated the facts as stated by Josiah Wilbarger, his brother, and confirmed by William Hornsby, who still lives, and others who are now dead." The vision which so impressed Mrs. Hornsby was spoken of far and wide throughout the country fifty years ago. Her earnest manner and perfect confidence that Wilbarger was still alive, made, in connection with her vision and its realization, a profound impression on the men present and they spoke of it everywhere. There were no telegraphs in those days, and no means of knowing that Margaret, the sister, had died seven hundred miles away, just the day before her brother was wounded. The story of her apparition, related before he even knew she was dead; her going in the direction of Hornsby's and Mrs. Hornsby's strange vision, recurring after slumber, present a mystery that made a deep impression and created a feeling of awe, which, after a lapse of a half century, it still inspires. No man who knew them ever questioned the veracity of either Wilbarger or the Hornsbys, and Mrs. Hornsby was loved and revered by all who knew her.

We leave to those more learned the task of explaining the strange coincidence of the visions of Wilbarger and Mrs. Hornsby. It must remain a marvel and a mystery. Such things are not accidents; they tell us of a spirit world and of a God who "moves in a mysterious way His wonders to perform." Josiah Wilbarger left a wife and five children. His widow married Tolbert Chambers, and was a second time left a widow and resided, in 1888, in Bastrop County, thirty-five miles below Austin. The oldest son was killed, many years after the death of his father, by the Indians in West Texas, as stated elsewhere in this book. Harvey, another son of Josiah, lived to raise a large family, then died. His widow and only son live in Bastrop County; one married daughter lives in Georgetown and another in Belton.

While in the foregoing account, we have two leading objectives: to give those strange visions that played a large part in that awful drama, and to give some faint idea of what those people had to endure. Further than this, there were some things transpiring about this time, leading to other events of so much interest that they cannot well be left out of this work of history of our Indian troubles.

In these frequent forays, the Comanches were carrying into an awful captivity many innocent women and children, whom they used as slaves and traded to the whites for merchandise and such other things as might please their fancy. This was a dreadful state of affairs, as it offered an inducement to the savages to continue their attacks upon the homes of the settlers and carry away captives. The torture to which they knew the captives were subjected to caused the friends and loved ones at home to make every effort, at whatever cost, to obtain the ransom of such captives. The Indians would pretend they desired a treaty of peace, in order to secure the opportunity to make and receive propositions for the ransom of the captives. Wilbarger, John Henry Brown and others mention some cases of this kind occurring prior to the Council House Fight at San Antonio. Among the most noted, perhaps, were the capture of Mrs. Crawford and that of Mrs. Webster.

Killing of the Goacher Family &
The Capture of Mrs. Crawford, 1840

Mr. Goacher was the leader in opening the trail to Stephen F. Austin's new colony in 1835, which is known as the Goacher Trail. He afterwards settled in Bastrop, prospered well, and soon became comfortably fixed. The family had a good log house built and felt rather secure from the Indians. They had opened up good farms, were quietly enjoying a good home and had a good living. This condition was not destined to last.

In 1837, while Mr. Goacher and his son-in-law were away from home in the forest gathering firewood, the house was surrounded by a band of Indians from two directions. One party came across three members of the family—a boy and the Goachers' married daughter, Jane Crawford and her little daughter—not far from the house. Fearing that they might give the alarm, the Indians speared the boy through the body and killed him. After scalping him, they took Jane as a captive and made a rush upon the house.

The Indians, seeing that there was no man present, made a violent attack. Mrs. Goacher, being a woman of great courage and having several loaded guns at hand, fired one after another into the savage foes. The Indians had expected no resistance, and the effect was to render them all the more desperate. They shot Mrs. Goacher so many times that she was almost covered with arrows, yet the brave woman stood at the door and defended her children to the last. Finally, one of the Indians who had a gun shot her, and she fell back upon the floor dead. This noble woman, regardless of the many and painful arrow wounds, regardless of certain death to herself, facing alone these horrible monsters in the defense of her children, furnishes a most heroic example of a mother's love, divine in its nature and overcoming completely that fear of death which so forcibly moves not only man himself, but all living creatures, to self-protection.

Mr. Goacher, his grandson and his son-in-law Crawford, hearing the firing, dropped everything, not even thinking of their guns, and ran to the assistance of the family. The only chance they had was to make a bold rush for the house and get possession of the guns. In making the attempt, the two men were killed and the grandson, finding himself alone, tried to escape but was caught by an Indian and given a terrible shaking. The boy caught one of the Indian's thumbs in his mouth and would not loosen his hold until the Indian had inflicted a fearful whipping upon him with a gun-stick. Another child, mortally wounded, crawled off and laid his head upon a stone and breathed his last.

This was one of the most dreadful massacres of which I have ever known. Judging from the courage shown by the entire family—father, mother, son-in-law and even the little boys—had it not been for the sudden surprise of the attack, they would have made a mighty effort, if not a successful defense of their home. But, being caught off their guard and unprepared for battle, resisting with the courage and desperation of the lion, they only succeeded in causing, perhaps, the greater slaughter.

Sad though one may feel at the thought of the father, mother and children, slain and bleeding from the ruthless murder...how much worse was the case of the daughter, seeing all this and beholding the vain efforts at rescue, torn from the bleeding side of her husband and children dying in her sight, and dragged away as a captive slave, and even worse, by those who had thus ruthlessly deprived her of all that she loved upon earth? The scene is heartrending indeed, and it seems enough to have crushed the stoutest courage, and rendered life unbearable.

Being held as captive for ransom and for the amusement of these dreadful savages, and forced to endure all the indignities and painful tortures to be invented by their evil natures, we find that there still burns within her a spark, as it were, of divinity itself—that unconquerable, unselfish and almost immortal mother's love for the baby girl, carried with her into captivity through all this trying ordeal.

Once, when the baby was fretting and crying in its mother's arms, the Indians became angered at her attentions to it, and determined to kill it. One snatched it from her and threw it into a deep pool of water nearby, intending to drown the little thing, and not taking into account the mother's love. Mrs. Crawford immediately plunged into the water for its rescue and, having succeeded, she was again and again, for the amusement of these fiends, caused to suffer the same intensely agonizing struggle to rescue her baby from a watery grave. As soon as she recovered the child, they threw it back into the water, and continued to repeat the performance until both mother and child were nearly exhausted.

At last, one of the savages, taking the child from its mother and drawing its little head backward, told another to cut its throat. The Indian started to do it, but the mother's love for the child was greater than her fear of death, and she seized a club and knocked the villain down. For her act, she could have expected nothing else than to be killed at once. On the contrary, though, they laughed lustily at the one who had received the blow and, one of them took the child, handed it to its mother and said, "Take it, damn you! Squaw heap brave!" They never tried to harm the baby after that, telling her to go take care of her papoose, that they wouldn't do it. Thus, by her brave and fearless conduct, she saved her dear little innocent child.

No doubt the Indians would have killed them both were it not for the hope of getting a large reward for them when they reached the trading house. After being kept a prisoner for almost two years, and having been treated in a manner too shameful to be related here, she and her child were carried to Coffee's trading house on the Red River, where they were bartered for large quantities of calico, blankets, beads, etc. These goods were furnished by Mr. Coffee, the trading agent and, having obtained their release from their cruel captors, he sent them under escort in control of a Mr. Spaulding, who conducted them safely through Texas and to Mrs. Crawford's old home.

Although she had successfully eluded the feathered shaft of the savage Indian through that dreadful massacre, on the way home Mrs. Crawford felt the tiny arrow from Cupid's bow and, succumbing to its influence, was united in marriage to Mr. Spaulding. They lived on and reared their family on the old Goacher homestead in Bastrop County, where they still reside. Thus it is seen that one of the prime motives the Indian had in taking these people as captives was to enrich their own supplies by trading them back to their friends. This was done in this and in other cases.

Capture & Escape of Mrs. Webster

James Webster was moving with a train of wagons to his league of land in Austin's Colony, and when out on the divide between the two San Gabriels, he discovered a large number of Comanches making their way toward white settlements. Thinking that the Indians had not seen the train, he turned towards the settlements. But the Indians had seen the train, followed it and camped not far from the camp of the train. Webster had his train arranged in a square for fear of an attack by them.

There were thirteen men in the train, as well as Mrs. Webster and her little daughter. At about the break of day the next morning, the Indians made their attack. The thirteen made a stubborn resistance until ten or eleven o'clock, when the last one of the white men fell. The Indians then rushed in upon the wagons and, after robbing them, rolled them together and burned them. Taking Mrs. Webster and her little daughter, together with whatever plunder they wanted, they fled into the mountains.

Mrs. Webster's account of her two year stay among the Indians is intensely interesting. She was often compelled to ride sixty or seventy miles in a day with neither food nor water, and sometimes for two or three days in succession. They begged her frequently to teach them how to make gunpowder, insisting that she knew how it was done or, if she did not, that she could explain to them how it was done and that they could then make it. To get rid of their continual annoyance, she told them that it was made somehow out of charcoal and sand. They soon filled several kettles with these ingredients. They boiled it with some water for a time and then, taking it out, they dried and pulverized it and tried to make it explode by throwing fire brands upon it. In the manufacture of it, they were very cautious to prevent it coming in contact with the fire, evidently thinking that they had at last discovered the true process for its manufacture. When they finally discovered that it could not be made to explode, they then said, "White man wouldn't let squaw know." They brought her paper money at different times, but to prevent them from using it in the purchase of firearms and ammunition, she told them that it was worthless and caused them to destroy thousands of dollars worth of it. In her story, Mrs. Webster gives an account of many rich gold and silver mines she had seen, and also of what appeared to her to be diamonds, but the Indians were very careful that she should not touch one of them.

For two long and weary years, she and her little daughter were kept as prisoners far back in the mountains in the Indian country but, finally, in the spring of 1840, there was a positive agreement between the Comanches and the Republic of Texas, that they each would bring in their prisoners and make a full exchange. The place appointed for this exchange was at the Council House in San Antonio. When the parties met, Colonel Fisher with his battalion and the commissioners, Colonel Cooke and General McLeod, represented the Republic. Twelve of the main chiefs of the Comanches, with a number of warriors and something like thirty or forty squaws and children, were also present.

Both parties had fully agreed to bring in all of their prisoners, but when the Indians came into the Council House, they had only Miss Lockhart. It was positively known that they had several others, particularly Mrs. Webster. The chiefs were then told that they were acting in bad faith, and that they themselves would now be held as prisoners until the others were brought in. This enraged the chiefs and, as we will see later on, resulted in a fight. As the Indians were coming to San Antonio, they left their families with a few warriors and Mrs. Webster, back about sixty miles.

That night Mrs. Webster, having learned from one of the squaws that the Indians did not intend to exchange herself and child, determined to make her escape if possible. So, the next night she took her little girl and slipped off into the darkness and, finding the trail that the Indians had made on their way to San Antonio, followed it very well all night. But when day began to dawn, concerned about being discovered, she went up on a hill where she could see the trail she had left and, hiding in the thick bushes, she remained there through the day. It was well up in the day when, as she expected, she saw some of the Indians following the trail that she had left, and late in the evening saw the same number returning just as they had gone, and was sure that they had given her up.

When the night returned, she began again her weary march, but her bare feet were terribly bruised and sore from the rocks and thorny brush along the way. Perseveringly, she worked her way along this perilous route, traveling by night and laying up in the day until she finally reached San Antonio a few days after the Council House Fight. She was perfectly naked, without even a rag of clothing on, and she quietly hid herself until it grew dark. She then slipped into a Mexican hut and made herself known. She was soon supplied with food and clothing and rendered as comfortable as possible. Poor suffering woman! Almost perishing with hunger, completely exhausted from creeping through the brush and briers, her feet worn by rocks and her flesh torn by thorns, she was certainly a pitiable sight.

But now all is changed and heaven seems at last to smile upon her, and she rejoices that she has finally escaped from that awful captivity. The Indians valued her too highly to bring her into the Council for exchange. They could use her to great advantage in dressing hides and doing other drudgery as a slave, and again could dispose of her to great advantage to the whites if opportunity offered, in securing such supplies as they might need. That a bright, intelligent woman, reared in culture and refinement, unaccustomed to even the drudgery of civilized life, could possibly survive these severe trials so long and still have the courage to make her escape through the wilds in the condition she was in, is simply remarkable and worth of the admiration of all.

Council House Fight at San Antonio

In reading the different histories written in regard to many of the events that occurred in the early settlement of the country, we find that they differ widely and sometimes materially in the details given, but in regard to the Council House Fight, they all seem to agree more perfectly than in regard to any other event of which I have read. John Henry Brown gives the names of those participating in that fight more fully than anyone else, but this he does in all of his work; and I must say here that he is very modest in claiming any honor for himself, always seeking to give others full credit for what they may have done, thereby showing a worthy spirit. The patriotism of the early settlers should not be treated lightly, nor forgotten by the present settlers, for it has won for them this great country, as a boon for them and their posterity; furnished homes for thousands of liberty-loving people, who should ever remember with suitable gratitude those, who, through great trials and suffering, have freed this beautiful land from the marauders and rendered it fit for the habitation of a happy people.

Early in 1840, when they heard that Colonel H. W. Carnes was at San Antonio, the Comanche chiefs sent a message indicating their desire for a treaty of peace with the whites. Although they had done this a number of times, and had as often broken their treaty, the people were so weary with the continuous warfare in which property was being destroyed, life unsafe and unpleasant, and their women and children being carried into captivity, that they had become anxious for some means to insure protection. They were again willing to give the Indians another trial at a treaty, though very doubtful of its results. Having little confidence in the sincerity of the Indians, they took every precaution to so conduct this treaty with them as to insure success.

The Indians, who presented the proposition to Colonel Carnes, were informed by him that if they would deliver all of the white prisoners whom they held in captivity, some thirteen in all, that they would have peace. They promised that they would do so at the next full moon. This information was communicated to the government, and Colonel Fisher was sent to San Antonio with a good force of men, ready to meet any emergency that might arise while the treaty was in progress. Colonel W. G. Cooke and General H. D. McLeod were appointed as commissioners to treat with the Indians.

According to the agreement, at the full moon in March, sixty-five Comanches, including men, women and children, came into San Antonio, ostensibly for the purpose of making a treaty of peace. Although they had promised to bring in all the prisoners, only Miss Matilda Lockhart was brought. It was known that they had several others, among them Mrs. Webster and her little girl. Twelve Comanche chiefs were met in the Council House by the commissioners, Col. Cooke and Gen. McLeod, with an interpreter.

When our commissioners asked where the prisoners were whom they had promised to deliver, Mukawarrah, the chief who made the promise at the first interview, replied, "We have brought the only one we have. The others are with other tribes." This was known to be false, for Miss Lockhart had said that she had seen several persons at their camp the evening before, and that the Indians intended to bring in one or two at a time in order to get a greater ransom for them. A long pause ensued, after which the chief inquired, "How do you like the answer?" No reply was made at first.

A messenger was sent immediately to Capt. Howard to bring his company into the council room. When the company had marched in, the interpreter was told to inform the chiefs that they would be held as prisoners until the other white captives were brought in. This the interpreter refused to convey, saying that the instant he told them, they would fight. The commissioner insisted and, placing himself near the door, the interpreter told the Indians and then left at once. As the interpreter predicted, the chiefs immediately prepared for action. Some strung their bows and arrows, and others drew their scalping knives. As the commissioners were retiring, one of the chiefs attempted to jump past the sentinel, who attempted to prevent him and was stabbed by the Indian. Capt. Howard was also stabbed. The fight then became general, and not until the last chief was slain did the conflict end.

The Indians who were outside, hearing the firing inside, immediately attacked the soldiers who were stationed around the house, and fought with desperation. Capt. Caldwell (known as Old Paint) was attacked by a powerful warrior and, being unarmed, was forced to protect himself by throwing rocks until someone shot and killed the Indian. In an adjoining room, Mr. Morgan was attacked by two Indians, but succeeded in killing them both. Capt. Dennington was killed by a squaw, who shot an arrow through his body. Judge Thompson was in the yard amusing himself setting up pieces of money for the little Indians to shoot arrows at. While thus engaged, he was killed by an arrow before he even realized he was in danger. Judge Hood was killed in the Council House.

Col. Wells rode into the plaza just as the fight commenced and a powerful Indian jumped up behind him and tried to throw him from the horse, but failing in that the Indian tried to grab the reins and make a run from the plaza. The Colonel tried to draw his revolver, but couldn't, as the Indian was holding his arms close to his body. After the two on the horse had circled around the plaza two or three times, one of the soldiers shot the Indian who, no doubt to the great satisfaction of Col. Wells, fell at once to the ground.

The Indians were finally forced by Capt. Redd and his company to take refuge in a stone house nearby, where all the warriors were shot except one who had ridden himself into another building. Every inducement was offered to this one to come from the house, but he would not do so. Finally, in order to induce him to come out, the men saturated a large ball of rags with turpentine and, setting it on fire, dropped it in upon him. He immediately sprang from the house and was shot to pieces by the soldiers. During the engagement, several of the warriors made their way across the San Antonio River, but were pursued and all were killed except one renegade Mexican who made his escape. All the warriors, thirty-three in number, with the three women and two children, were killed and twenty-seven women and children were made prisoners. The Texans had seven killed and eight wounded.

After the fight, a squaw was sent to the Comanches to inform them that if they would bring in all their prisoners, that an exchange would still be made. After the lapse of several days, a body of Comanches made their appearance some distance from San Antonio, yet in sight of the town, and raised a white flag. The white men met them with a white flag and learned that the Indians had their prisoners ready this time. The exchange was soon made. When the prisoners were exchanged, the rejoicing on both sides was almost overwhelming. The Indians went back to their mountain home, only to formulate plans of revenge upon the white men by the invasion of the settlements. They, no doubt, were influenced to a great extent by one of the Mexican officers who was then working in that interest. It was not long before an army of from eight hundred to one thousand warriors strong was on the march for the settlements.

Sacking of Linnville

This was the first regular invasion made upon the white settlements of Texas, by the united tribes of Comanches and Kiowas. There were a number of marauding parties which had come into the State for the purpose of plundering, killing beeves and capturing prisoners to be ransomed by their friends.

The Council House Fight brought change in the policies of both the white man and the Indian. The various rewards that had been, from time to time, paid for the ransom of the various prisoners that had been taken captives by the Indians, had only operated as an incentive for them to capture others for the same purpose. The tortures to which the prisoners were exposed was partly to cause their friends to become more anxious to ransom them. The people were almost driven to desperation, and were determined to protect themselves against the red rascals, and make them afraid to come into the settlements. The Comanches and Kiowas were living back somewhat to the northwest of San Antonio and, after the Council House Fight, they seemed to avoid the town and began their invasion in that vast country toward the southeast. This afforded them the opportunity to go around the dreaded San Antonio, through an uninhabited part of the country, and suddenly and unexpectedly attack the people living along the coast.

About the full of the moon in August of 1840, they were on the march for Victoria with nearly a thousand warriors, some old men and a few squaws. They reached that place on the 6th of the month and, with the intention of wreaking vengeance for the death of their chiefs at San Antonio, they plunged unexpectedly upon that quiet coastal village, and dealt death and destruction all around them. The people were wholly unprepared for the attack and the consternation that prevailed is difficult to describe.

Quite a number of people were killed and wounded, while a number took refuge in the strongest buildings and barricaded themselves until the savages left. The Indians carried away with them thousands of head of cattle, horses and mules, and camped for the night not many miles from the town.

Being so successful at Victoria gave them the courage to further pillage, and they determined to capture and destroy the seaport town of Linnville, about fifty miles from Victoria. On the way, they came across and captured Mrs. Crosby and her child.

Early in the morning of August 8th, some of the people of Linnville observed a great cloud of dust rising, but thought that it was a large herd of horses coming from Mexico for trading purposes. The Comanches, by leaning to the sides of their horses, had kept themselves well concealed from the unsuspecting citizens of the town. The great fear and consternation which fell upon them when the presence of the Indians was discovered cannot be imagined.

All at once, one thousand red savages rise from the sides of what they had thought was only a bunch of Mexican ponies for market. The Indians rushed in with all their hideous yelling upon a defenseless town, with its people engaged in the quiet pursuit of their ordinary avocations, and without scarcely a word of warning began that fearful massacre. The first thought of the people was the water, and men, women and children made a rush for the boats lying in the shallow water nearby. This scene, amid this great confusion, will never be forgotten by those who survived it.

The horrible war-whoop of the savages, with the shrieks of the woman and children, mingled with the groans of the wounded and dying were appalling in the extreme. The people offered no resistance and sought safety only in flight. The savages followed them, even into the water, killing and capturing many of them. Capt. Walls, the collector of customs, was killed and his young bride caught upon the water and carried away as a captive. Several negroes were killed, but the greater portion of the people, having reached the boats and pushed out into deep water in time, were saved. All who failed to do so were either killed or carried away as captives. The stores of the town were all pillaged and, taking whatever they desired and catching hundreds of mules, the Indians packed the animals with their plunder and then decorated them with ribbons and calicoes of the gayest colors. There were also ribbons streaming from their own, as well as their horses', heads. Having completed their pillaging and taken everything that they could carry away with them, they set fire to this beautiful little village and destroyed, in sight of the people in the boats, all of the homes. Here the Indians remained until in the night some time, when they started back whence they came.

Battle of Plum Creek - August 1840

When the Indians left Linnville and started back, they had with them between three and four thousand horses and mules. As soon as they had left, the people of Linnville sent messengers to Guadalupe, Gonzales, Lavaca and Colorado settlements to notify the citizens, and it was not long before the people were rallying from every direction. Of course, such an invasion as this by such a large number of Indians so destructive in its results had aroused everyone who had the least bit of patriotism, and everyone was willing to help repel and teach these bloody-handed, treacherous thieves that if they could not be trusted in a treaty, they could be driven out of the country and made afraid to return in the manner they had come in upon these unsuspecting people.

A man named Z. N. Morrell, a Baptist preacher and a man of great courage, happened to be returning to Bastrop from the Guadalupe where he had been improving a farm. While passing over the divide towards the Lavaca River, on the 10th of August about mid-day, he crossed the trail the Indians had made en route to Victoria and Linnville. Although he was at the time driving an ox team, he traveled thirty miles in twelve hours, so eager was he to communicate this news to Col. Burleson and the people of the Colorado valley. By sunrise the next morning, Morrell was at La Grange and had met Col. Burleson, and reported to him what he had seen. Burleson at once mounted his horse and began immediately to organize a company for the purpose of meeting the enemy.

Wilbarger, in his book, quotes from the preacher Morrell and says, "By the time we were mounted and ready to start, an express man came in sight with a paper fluttering in his hand. He presented the paper, which read about thus: 'General: The Indians have sacked and burned the town of Linnville and carried off several prisoners. We made a draw fight with them at Cassa Blanca, but could not stop them. We want to fight them before they reach the mountains.

We have sent express men up the Guadalupe. (Signed) Ben McCulloch.'"

It seems that a few of the men from Gonzales, Guadalupe and Lavaca had gathered together and had attacked the Indians as they were marching back across the country, but they were not strong enough to do much to them. As we will learn further on, Ben McCulloch was not easily discouraged nor did he turn back on account of the superior number of Indians, but by whipping around them, he fell in with Capt. Caldwell (Old Paint), who was in command of a company of thirty-seven men. There were two other small companies under the commands of Captains Ward and Bird. The entire number was not far from ninety men. These three companies camped on the night of the eleventh at the place appointed for them to rendezvous, where they expected to meet the Indians.

Preacher Morrell, in speaking of the movements of Col. Burleson and himself, says: "We made our way up the Colorado valley as rapidly as we could to Bastrop, notifying everyone as we went. At Bastrop, Col. Burleson called a council, and it was agreed that the enemy should be intercepted at Good's, on Plum Creek, twenty miles below Austin."

The three small companies who had gone into camp were keeping a sharp lookout for the enemy when, early on the morning of the 12th, Caldwell's spies reported that the Indians were approaching and were in sight. Up to this time, Col. Burleson, with his one hundred men and thirteen Tonkawa Indians under the command of their gallant old chief, Placido, had not arrived. Old Paint was there, though, and whenever he was where there were Indians, there was pretty sure to be a fight. It mattered little how much they outnumbered him.

It is not an uncommon thing at any time when old Texans get together to hear the question, "Do you remember Old Paint's speech at Plum Creek?" In order that the few but impressive words of that grand old warrior may not be forgotten, we reproduce them here as nearly as we can. He said: "Boys, the Indians number about one thousand. They have our women and children captives. We are only eighty-five strong, but I believe we can whip them. Shall we fight? What do you say?" It is pointless to say that the answer all down the line was, "Yes! Fight 'em! Fight 'em!"

On the evening before, Felix Houston, who was senior in command, had arrived and was placed in command of the companies. While the plan of attack was being arranged, Col. Burleson came up with his men, and they were soon thrown into line. The Indians were now moving on the prairie in full view. It must have been a strange sight—a thousand red warriors with three or four thousand horses, and three or four hundred mules, packed with goods and plunder—marching along in full view of this band of Texans, only two hundred strong but too brave and too strong to be intimidated by such a bunch of Comanches.

When Col. Burleson arrived, he was given command of the right wing. Capt. Caldwell had the left and Monroe Hardeman (Old Gotch) was to bring up the rear. The Indians were at once thrown into line by their chief who lead the invasion. "The enemy," says Preacher Morrell, "were induced to keep at a distance and delay the fight in order that the pack mules might be driven ahead." During this delay, several of their chiefs performed some startling feats. According to previous arrangement, our men waited for the Indians to get beyond the point of timber, before making the general charge.

"One of the chiefs, who was mounted on a fine horse which had about twenty feet of red ribbon tied to his tail, attracted a great deal of attention. He was dressed in an elegant suit of clothes taken from some of the stores at Linnville, with the fine broadcloth coat on backwards, showing the shiny buttons at his back. When he first made his appearance, he was carrying a large opened umbrella. He with others would charge toward us and shoot their arrows, doing no damage, then fall back. This was done several times in range of our guns, but it was soon discovered that this chief wore a shield for, although our men took good aim, their balls glanced. An old Texans from Lavaca asked to have his horse held and, getting as near the place where they wheeled as was safe and waiting patiently until they came, fired and brought the chief to the ground."

The effect of the chief's downfall was to check the Indians' demonstrations, which they had continued, although several had previously met the same fate. They persisted in their efforts to remove the chief to the rear, although several of them were killed in the attempt, and at last they succeeded in carrying him back. Gen. Houston, who had suggested the delay in making the attack and whose men were suffering during the constant firing of the enemy while their chiefs were performing, was now told by Ben McCulloch that this was not the way to fight Indians. Houston ordered an immediate charge.

Those two hundred men, afire with the thought of revenge for the murder of those who fell at Victoria and Linnville, now dashed forward under their gallant leaders and with a wild yell that made the earth tremble, accompanied by the brave Placido and his thirteen indomitable followers, the faithful friends of the white man, dealt death and destruction on all sides. Placido and his men, before going into battle, had tied white handkerchiefs around their arms to distinguish them from the Comanches.

The Indians could not long withstand this furious onslaught of the white man, and soon their rout became a general stampede. It was a running fight for twelve or fifteen miles. The pack mules and loose horses were principally abandoned and then, in their flight, they seemed to lose all order. Every fellow tried to take care of himself, and was a self-appointed agent to look after the welfare of his own scalp. Ben McCulloch, Miller and C. C. DeWitt, seeing five Indians running off, pursued and killed every one of them.

John Henry Brown, whose history I follow and compare with that of others as well as other data, was too modest to claim any credit for himself when telling of this fight. I'm told that in a hand-to-hand fight, Brown killed one of the most noted of the chiefs. At the time the chief was killed, he wore a cap made of the skin off of the head of a buffalo, with the horns attached. John Henry Brown estimated that about eighty-five Indians were killed and a large number wounded. None of the white men were killed, but several were wounded. Gen. Houston does not place the number of Indians killed quite so high as Brown does, although both men were present and engaged in the battle. Just before the Indians began their precipitate retreat, they killed Mrs. Crosby, whom they had captured as a prisoner before.

Mrs. Watts was shot in the breast with an arrow and was found soon afterwards by Preacher Morrell, who says, "Just before the retreat began, I heard the scream of a female voice in a bunch of bushes close by. Approaching, I found a lady trying to pull out an arrow that was firmly affixed in her breast. She proved to be Mrs. Watts whose husband was killed at Linnville. Dr. Brown of Gonzales was at once sent for to attend her wound. Nearby me, I also discovered a white woman and a negro woman, both dead. These had all been shot with arrows when the howl went up and the retreat commanded.

"Dr. Brown, who had been sent for, soon made his appearance, and as he approached, I succeeded in loosening the hands of Mrs. Watts from the arrow. The dress and flesh on each side of the arrow were cut and an effort was made to extract it. But the poor sufferer would seize the hands of the doctor and scream so that the doctor would stop, but Dr. Brown made one last effort and succeeded. 'My blankets,' says Dr. Brown, 'were spread on the ground and as she rested thereon with my saddle for a pillow, she was composed and soon rejoiced at her escape.' Death would have been to her a preferable fate than that of crossing the mountains with these savages. She had ridden a pack mule all the way from the coast and when they would stop, she was required for their amusement to read the books they had stolen. She lived many years and died at Port Lavaca in 1878."

Thus ended the battle of Plum Creek, on August 12, 1840. The Indians, instead of keeping up their policy of invading in overwhelming numbers as it seemed from this raid was their intention, were taught such a lesson by the results of this battle that they abandoned the idea and never tried it again. Had they done so, the white men could have been better enabled to engage them in battle and, being so far superior in actual warfare, would soon have exterminated the Indians. The savages thereafter returned to their old way of slipping around like the lobo and the coyote wolf, to kill and steal and slip away again without ever being caught. In this way, they were a continual annoyance for years after since the white man, being domestic in his habits of life and his time being precious to him, could not waste his life chasing the wild Indian over the prairies.

The Raid on Parker's Fort

In 1835, Parker's Fort was established on the Navasota River, near where the present town of Groesbeck is now located. It is beautifully situated on a natural elevation near the edge of the river bottom. Well planned and well built was this fort where the first settlement of the Parker family in Texas was made, with every available means of protection from the enemy, the red man, in use.

Here, with his daughter, his son-in-law Plummer, and their fifteen-month-old baby, Mr. John Parker and a number of friends settled. They immediately set about making improvements, carrying on farming and stock raising. After about a year had elapsed, one balmy May day, while the men were peacefully following their pursuits on the farm, a large body of Comanche and Kiowa Indians very suddenly and unexpectedly appeared. They killed quite a number.

Mrs. Plummer and her babe, with several other women, John Parker and his sister Cynthia Ann, were captured. The men, who had taken weapons to their work, were unaware of the fate of their families until the Indians had obtained complete possession. So overwhelmed were the white men in numbers that they were unable to liberate their loved ones, or drive back the Indians. However, by making repeated attacks, the men gave several women and children the opportunity to escape to the brush on the creek nearby. The Indians charged upon them, but as the men would present their guns, they would stop and wheel back. Here Abraham Anglin, Silas Bates and David Faulkenberry, all armed, along with Plummer who was unarmed, came upon the scene. This caused the Indians to withdraw their attack. One old warrior, before turning back, ran up on them, but Mrs. Parker's dog grabbed the Indian's horse by the nose, causing him to rear and plunge into a ditch.

The white party made their escape to the timber in safety but as they were passing the place where they had been at work that morning, Plummer seemed suddenly to regain his senses and realize that his wife and child had not been found. Asking where they were, and receiving no reply, he turned back, still unarmed, to search for them.

The rest of the party made their way to a place of comparative safety in the thick brush, and stopped for a council. They decided to attempt a march to Fort Houston, ninety miles distant. Anglin and Faulkenberry, after spending the night in the brush, started the next morning at daybreak, back to the scene of the struggle, to take care of any who might have been wounded and needed attention, or perhaps locate those who may have made an escape and were in hiding. As they were returning, they passed Faulkenberry's cabin and, here, Anglin says, he beheld for the first time a ghost. On near approach, however, it proved to be Grandmother Parker. She had been severely wounded and stripped of her clothes, had barely escaped death in the previous day's struggle and had crawled to this place. They gave her some bedclothes and provided for her comfort as best as they could until they should return. She remained hidden there while they went into the fort. Upon reaching that place, they found no one alive. Some of the horses were there. Dogs, cattle, horses and hogs seemed to realize that something was seriously wrong, and were making such a great noise that the party feared that the Indians might still be lurking nearby, and did not remain long. Returning to where they had left Grandmother Parker in concealment, they took her with them to their hiding place in the brush.

To give a more definite idea of the terrible ordeal through which these people passed, we will give the account as given in J. W. Parker's history:

"When we started off to Fort Houston, I took one child in my arms and another on my shoulders, and led the march. The other grown people did the same and followed. Thus our party, numbering eighteen, started on this long journey through the tangled brush and briars. Our progress was necessarily very slow, as most of our number were barefooted, and the children almost unclothed. We traveled until about three o'clock when, feeling somewhat secure, we decided to stop till morning to take a much needed rest; but as we came to the edge of the prairie, so many Indian tracks were found, and so much circling and maneuvering had been done, that we felt convinced that they were searching for us. We hastily made our way back into the thickets and briars, for even if they did tear our flesh and pierce our feet, they might save our lives and scalps. As our party struggled along, they could almost be trailed by the stains from their bleeding feet.

"By the evening of the second day, so great was the suffering from hunger and fatigue, especially among the mothers with infants, that hope of completing our journey almost failed. Providence favored us here in a way we had not experienced before, but now welcomed heartily. As we were immediately upon the bank of the river, a polecat appeared. I ran to catch him. He jumped into the river just as I caught him by the tail and held him under the water until he was drowned. We made a fire, cooked and ate our meat and resumed our journey. This was our only sustenance until the fourth day, when we had the good fortune to capture another polecat and some terrapins.

"By the fifth day, we were so completely exhausted and so nearly famished that a continuation of our journey seemed impossible. Coming to a place with which I was familiar, and knowing that it was only thirty-five miles from Fort Houston, it was decided that I should go for assistance. Leaving Mr. Dwight in charge of the women and children, I set out early the next morning to the Fort. I reached there in the evening, having traveled thirty-five miles in eight hours. Recalling this occasion, it has always been a wonder to me that I was able to make this trip, as I had eaten nothing for five days and nights, having given my share of food to the perishing women and children. The thought of the poor sufferers I had left behind me, dependent on this effort, nerved me to the arduous task, and God gave me the strength to perform it. It is often said, 'Where there is a will there is a way.' Such is not always the case, for Napoleon had a will at Waterloo, but there was no way.

Love finds a way. Those I loved were there, and I found the way. Upon reaching the Fort, the first man to meet me was Capt. Carter, who at once had five horses ready. He, with Mr. Courtney, accompanied me on my return to the suffering party. When we reached them, the women and children were placed on the horses, and by midnight our journey was ended. Arriving at Capt. Carter's, each one was cared for as their need required. All that kind friends with benevolent hands and loving hearts can do was done.

"On the following morning, Plummer, my son-in-law, came in, having found no trace of his wife and child. About noon, twelve men set out for Parker's Fort to bury the dead. There in their quiet graves, unmarked by marble slab or anything to indicate their last resting place, they lie—but are not forgotten. Peace to their ashes. They mingled their tears with blood, as sufferers for this great country; and those who enjoy its prosperity should know that it was, as it were, purchased with the tears and blood of these patriots.

"Our party, at last recovering from the effects of this horrible journey, were reassured of their safety and most of them returned to their homes at Parker's Fort."

The Captives of Parker's Fort

After leaving Parker's Fort, the Comanche and Kiowa Indians remained together. They camped about midnight on a high prairie. After disposing of their horses for the night, they put out their pickets; they then brought their prisoners, each tied hand and foot with strong rawhide thongs that almost cut into their flesh, and placed them facedown in a circle. The Indians then began their hideous war dance around them, yelling, trampling upon them, and beating them with their bows until the blood covered the ground around them. Here, prostrate, these poor captives were left until morning. Such sufferings cannot be described, for words are inadequate to picture the horrors of the scene. Mrs. Kellogg was fortunate to fall into the hands of the Keechi Indians and, after about six months, was purchased by the Delawares. They delivered her to Sam Houston for the price which they paid for her: one hundred and fifty dollars.

Mrs. Plummer remained a captive for almost two years. Her own account gives a faint idea of what she suffered during this time. She says:

"I was taken away back among some very high mountains, and spent July and most of August there. It was so cold I suffered more than I had ever suffered before. I had very little covering for my feet, and but little clothing for my body. I had a certain number of buffalo hides to dress each day, and had to mind the horses at night, often having to take the buffalo hides with me to finish while I minded the horses. Although my feet would get frostbitten, I did not complain for fear of punishment. In about what I suppose was October, I gave birth to my second son, a very beautiful, strong child. It was impossible for me to have any comforts for myself or baby; yet the Indians were not as harsh in their treatment as I had expected them to be.

"I was apprehensive for the safety of my child from the first. I had now been with them six months and had learned their language. I would beseech my mistress what to do to save my child. She would always turn a deaf ear to my pleadings. My baby was six months old when my master, thinking, I suppose, that it interfered too much with my work, determined to put it out of the way. One very cold morning, five or six Indians came to where I was suckling my baby. As soon as they came, I felt sick at heart. My fears were aroused for the safety of my child, and these fears were well founded.

"One of the Indians grabbed my baby by the throat and choked it until it was apparently dead, and then threw it up and let it fall a number of times, and gave it back to me. I had been constantly weeping, but now my grief was so great my tears just stopped, and as I watched him, I thought I saw signs of life. But as soon as the Indians discovered that my child was yet alive, they tore it from my bosom and knocked me down. They tied a rawhide rope around its neck and threw it into a bunch of prickly pears, until its tender flesh was torn from its body. One of the Indians who was mounted then tied the end of the rope to his saddle and galloped around in a circle until my innocent little child was not only dead, but torn to pieces. One of them untied the rope and threw the remains in my lap. I dug a hole in the earth and buried them. After performing the last sad rites for the lifeless remains of my dear babe, I sat down and gazed with a feeling of relief over the little grave I had made for, it, in the wilderness, and could only say with David of old, 'You cannot come to me, but I can go to you.' And then, and even now, as I record these lines, giving an account of the dreadful scene, I rejoice that my babe had passed from the sorrows and sufferings of this world. I shall never hear its dying cry anymore, and fully believing in the imputed righteousness of God in Christ Jesus, I feel that my babe is with kindred spirits in the eternal world of joys. O, that my Savior may keep me through life's short journey, and bring me to dwell with my children in the realms of eternal bliss!"

Mrs. Plummer has gone to rest and, no doubt, her hopes have been realized. After this, she was given as a servant to a very cruel old squaw who treated her in a very brutal manner. Her son had been carried off by another party to the far West. She supposed her husband and father were killed. Her infant was dead, and death to her would have been a sweet relief. Life was a burden. She resolved no longer to submit to the intolerant old squaw. One day when the two were at a distance from the camp, but in sight of it, her mistress attempted to beat her with a club. Determined not to submit to this, she wrenched the club from the old squaw and knocked her down with it. The Indians, who had witnessed the whole proceeding from the camp, came running up, shouting at the top of their voices. Mrs. Plummer expected to killed, but they patted her on the shoulders, crying, "Buena! Buena!" (Good! Good! or Well done!) She now fared much better, soon became a favorite and was called The Fighting Squaw.

Mrs. Plummer was eventually rescued through the agency of some Mexican Santa Fe traders, by a noble-hearted American merchant, William Donahue. She was purchased so far north in the Rocky Mountains that it required seventeen days to bring her to Santa Fe. She was at once made a member of the family of her benefactor, where she received the kindest care and attention. Ere long, she accompanied Mrs. and Mr. Donahue to Independence, Mo., where she had the pleasure of meeting her brother-in-law, L. D. Nixon, who brought her back to her friends in Texas.

During her stay with the Indians, she had many thrilling experiences, which she often related to her friends. She told of going into a cave with an old squaw where she found a large diamond, but was forced to give it up. She was away on this terrible trip just twenty-one months and, on her return, said she never knew what became of her son who was two years old when they were captured, for she saw him only briefly after they were captured. She dictated a book in which was given a very graphic history of her capture and the thrilling incidents of her captivity and a history of her father's frontier life, which is of interest but is out of print and can hardly be obtained. In this book, she tells the last she saw of Cynthia Ann and John Parker. Mrs. Plummer died just one year after reaching her home. Her son who was captured with her was ransomed and taken to Fort Gibson in 1842, and reached home in 1843 in the charge of his grandfather. He became a very respectable citizen of Anderson County.

Still left in captivity, Cynthia Ann and John Parker were, as was subsequently learned, held by separate bands of Comanches. Being thus separated, they both forgot their native language and became thorough Comanches. It seems that as the long years crept slowly by, they forgot all about their home and their loved ones. But it does seem that the awful scenes of the massacre would have been indelibly impressed upon their minds, even though they had no one with them with whom to talk of the past.

John Parker grew to manhood and went on a raid down on the Rio Grande into Old Mexico. The party captured a Mexican girl of great beauty with whom John fell in love at first sight, and it seems that his affection was reciprocated by the Donna Juanita. Soon they were engaged to be married. Each day as their cavalcade moved on, they would ride side by side and talk of their future life. Just at this time, John was stricken with smallpox, and had been left to live or die, as the case may be. The little Aztec beauty refused to leave her lover, insisting on being left to take care of him. The Indians very reluctantly consented. With Juanita to cheer and care for him, John finally recovered, after which they became man and wife with as little ceremony as had Adam and Eve. Donna Juanita had great influence over her lover and soon induced him to abandon the roaming life of the Comanche and seek the quiet comforts of civilization. "Settling in the far West," says Thrall's *History of Texas*, "they built a nice cattle ranch and were well-to-do. When the war began, John joined a Mexican company in the Confederate service, but would never leave the State of Texas, where he made a gallant soldier." Wilbarger's history says that he was across the Rio Grande in the edge of Mexico at the time he wrote, in 1888.

CYNTHIA ANN PARKER

There is no individual in all the annals of Indian depredations on the frontiers of Texas that is of greater interest to the writer than Cynthia Ann Parker. This is not only on account of her being connected with a very prominent family of our state and being the wife of a prominent Indian chief, and the mother, too, of one of the most sagacious and influential Indian chiefs that has ever been known, but also on account of her devotion to her Indian family, her coolness and presence of mind when overtaken by her captors. I knew, personally, when she was captured, and of her return afterward. Her quiet submission and readiness to learn things that pertained to civilized life, after having been taken from it at the age of nine years and deprived of its blessings for twenty years thereafter, shows her to be a character very unique indeed.

Four long years had elapsed from the time she was mercilessly torn from the fond embrace of mother and friends and carried away into a captivity worse than death, and during all this time she had received no tidings from her friends at home, nor had they heard anything from her. Many efforts had been made to recover her, but they met with no success. In 1840, Col. Lee Williams, accompanied by a man named Stout and a Delaware Indian guide named Jack Harry, went with some goods loaded on pack mules, for the purpose of trading with the Indians. Far up on the Canadian River, they met with Pahaucha's band of Comanches, with whom they were peaceably trading. Cynthia Ann Parker was with this tribe. She was not nearly fourteen years old and, having been with the Indians nearly five years, had not seen a white person for that duration. After finding the family into which she had been adopted, Col. Williams proposed to barter for her. The old Comanche told him that all the goods he had would not redeem her and, says Col. Williams, the fierceness of that old Indian's countenance showed that it would be dangerous to make any further propositions of the kind.

Through the influence of old Pahaucha, the chief, the old Indian was persuaded to let Col. Williams and his men see her. She came and sat by the root of a tree. While their presence was surely a very happy event to this poor, stricken captive who, during her long captivity had become inured to hardships and perhaps had formed some ties of friendship, when they tried to talk with her she refused to speak a word. As she sat there, apparently deep in thought, perhaps of the faraway friends and her great grief at the time of her capture, the men tried earnestly to induce her to give some expression. They told her of former playmates and dear friends, and asked for some message from her to them. But she, having no doubt been commanded to silence, answered not a word, evidently fearing punishment if she did. She showed as little anxiety as possible, but the great anxiety of her mind was clearly portrayed in the gentle quivering of her lips, which showed that she still, to some extent, had some tender and humane feelings.

The years continued to roll slowly by until she reached womanhood. She must have been a charming woman for her situation, as one of the leading chiefs and a great warrior became infatuated with her. Thus she became the bride of the noted Peta Nocona, who was the peer of any Indian chief of his day, not excepting the great chief, Big Foot, who was slain in a hand-to-hand conflict by Col. S. P. Ross. As the wife of Peta Nocona, she bore him children and evidently loved him. When a group of hunters, among whom were personal friends of her family, were in Peta Nocona's camp, they recognized her and talked with her about returning to civilization. She shook her head and, pointing to the little naked children sporting at her feet and then to the Indian chief lying asleep in the shade nearby, she said, "He is good and kind to me and my children, who are his, and I cannot leave them." Of course, we can only think of him as a cruel, dusky monster and tyrant who would lord it over his pale-faced wife, but she honored him as the father of her children.

Cynthia Ann was no doubt present at many of the Indian battles and massacres on the border, and received of the spoils that were taken; at the devastation of the coast where whole towns, such as Linnville, were completely sacked of everything; on the pell-mell retreat up the Guadalupe and Colorado before the notorious Texas Rangers, under Moor and McCulloch. The excitements of the chase and the occasional successes on their raids engaged her attention and displaced thoughts of her once affectionate and happy surroundings. Impressions of early childhood began to fade until they were almost obliterated from her mind, seldom to return. Even when the Indians came in, flaunting the scalps of those of her own blood kindred, and while the others were rejoicing, she too, no doubt, joined in the exultations, thinking only of her present companions with whom were all of her hopes for the future as well as her associations. Especially was this so after her marriage and the birth of her children, to whom she was so much attached and in whose welfare she was so greatly interested. She evidently looked to her chief with great pride, for he was a leader and commander of superior ability.

Now, many years after the taking of Cynthia Ann and John Parker, back at their old home of Parker's Fort, things have changed. Isaac Parker was in the legislative councils of his state when, in 1846, it passed into the Union of States, and the powerful arm of the Union was thrown around our once almost helpless people. Their homes are now more secure, and general prosperity has come to our whole land. Where once the wild savages held sway and their hideous yells startled many a poor, innocent family, and where the shrieks and groans of their wounded and dying victims were heard, now the sweet, joyful songs and laughter of childhood and youth cheer the hearts of the people. Though long years have crept slowly by, Cynthia Ann and her brother are not forgotten, but kind and loving friends still search for them in every possible way—by adventures among the savages, making inquiries and by direct attack in battle.

Battles on the Canadian River

In 1858, I lived in Ellis County where, at Waxahachie, a company was formed to accompany Colonels Ford, Ross and others high up on the South Canadian, to the very home of the Comanches. I was, at that time, only eighteen years of age but very anxious to go with them. Although I had been accustomed to riding horseback after cattle on the prairies for nearly ten years, my friends thought it not best for me to go, and so I remained at home. Many of our young men did go, and through them I gathered a great deal of information about their trip. I learned from them of Old Iron Jacket, who wore a coat of scaled mail, on account of which he received the name. He claimed that his life was charmed, that bullets swerved around him and that he caused them to turn by blowing his breath at them as they came toward him. He was what the Indians called a medicine man and they believed he was invulnerable to bullets, but as to this claim we shall see further on.

Peta Nocona was the head chief and in command when Ford's company reached the vicinity of the Indian camp. No doubt, at that time, Cynthia Ann Parker and her boys were with him. On approaching the Washita, the helpful Tonkawa Indians numbering over a hundred and well armed with rifles, under the leadership of Chief Placido, reported that the camp of the Comanches was in the immediate vicinity. Col. Ford and Capt. S. P. Ross (father of ex-governor L. S. Ross) stood on a ridge and watched the Comanches running buffalo. They seemed to be wholly unaware of the presence of two hundred dreaded white men and the Tonkawas, bitter foes of the Comanches.

That night, the Tonkawa spies reconnoitered the camp of the enemy and, at daylight, the Tonks lead the advance on the Comanches. This was done in order to deceive the Comanches as to who was to be in the fight, which was short and decisive. The women and children were all captured, but not a single warrior surrendered, preferring death to capture.

After the sun was shining in its full strength over the hilltops, the Rangers and the Tonks came in full view of another camp across the Canadian River in a beautiful valley. A lone Indian was seen coming up in front of them and, being pursued by them, he led them to a safe crossing on this boggy stream. He fled into the village and gave the other Indians the alarm. Soon, four hundred warriors stood in line of battle between the enemy and their women and children.

Col. Ford formed his men in a few minutes, putting the Tonks on the right so that they might begin the attack in order to deceive the Comanches in regard to the nature of their arms, as well as the foe they had to meet. Pahehita Onasha, Iron Jacket, rode up and down between the lines of battle, defying his enemies, and several shots were fired at him without effect until, finally, Tonkawa Jim took a careful shot at him with his rifle and off Iron Jacket rolled. His warriors rushed around him. Iron Jacket never tried to rise—he was dead. At the same time, the Rangers and Tonks together made a terrific charge and, after a few discharges of their rifles, the Comanches were completely routed. The women and children, as well as the men, commenced the mournful wail of defeat, and abandoned the field to the victorious Rangers and Tonks. They fell back in sufficient order for the women and children to make their escape. To the captives of the early morning, taken by the Tonks, they now added about four hundred horses, besides a large amount of plunder in hides, meat and other things.

The fight was soon over. The Indians scattered off north and west, and the Rangers and Tonks came back to the battleground, one or two at a time until midday. Soon after noon, Peta Nocona, with four or five hundred of his warriors, came over the hills from up the Canadian, marching to the rescue of the camp that had just been taken. He had evidently met some of the escaping Indians, and his keen hearing had detected the roar of the morning's battle. With Cynthia Ann, his wife, and his two boys at his side, he was rushing to the relief of his people. As his men came up, they fell into position until their line reached for some distance, giving the appearance of a large force.

About this time, among the very last to return from the pursuit of those who had fled from the morning's battle, came Capt. Ross who asked Col. Ford what his purpose was in forming his men in line of battle. Col. Ford had only to point toward the hills about a mile distant, where Peta Nocona's line could be seen. Notwithstanding the defeat in the morning, they were now ready and anxious for another affray. Peta Nocona was a great warrior and knew little of defeat but he moved cautiously, evidently intending at some advantageous moment, to spring upon his enemy like a panther and destroy him before he could recover. In full view of each other stood the two lines of battle, with the Indians largely in excess of numbers, while the Rangers and Tonks, with their rifles and plenty of ammunition, had the advantage in arms.

Col. Ford again sent Placido with his Tonkawas in advance, which had the effect of drawing the Comanches down into the edge of the valley where the Rangers then advanced upon them. In the midst of the fierce battle that was raging between the Tonks and Comanches, the Rangers under Lieut. Nelson, by a rapid flanking attack, surprised the Comanches and caused them to beat a retreat. A running fight ensued for several miles, in which Peta Nocona so maneuvered his men that all the women and children effected their escape. At one point, the Rangers thought they would be able to capture all the women and children, but they were mistaken. Col. Ford, realizing that his men and his horses were greatly fatigued, ordered a halt and return to the captured village, where they gathered the trophies of victory and returned to the settlements. The coat of mail which they took from the body of Iron Jacket, together with other trophies of victory, was placed in the archives of the State at Austin.

Before closing this sketch, we cannot refrain from a word of praise for Placido and his Tonkawa soldiers, who were always true and had here fought so bravely.

Battle of the Wichita Mountains

Notwithstanding the terrible defeat by Colonel Ford and S. P. Ross at the Canadian River, the Comanches were soon as troublesome as ever. Major Van Dorn was ordered to go, with four companies of United States soldiers in company with Ross' Indian scouts, on a raid upon the hostile Indians. They went out into the Indian country and established a fort by building a stockade in which to keep their mules and horses when it became necessary.

The Tonkawa scouts were sent out to look for the Comanches. Young Sul Ross, scarcely twenty-one years of age and on leave from college, was in charge of the Indian scouts. In a short time, the scouts returned and reported a large Comanche camp near the Wichita Mountains, about ninety miles distant from the fort, and that the Indians seemed ignorant of the proximity of the white soldiers.

Leaving a strong guard at the fort, the four companies, together with the company of Indian scouts, started for the Comanche camp. They arrived in sight of the camp on the third morning, just as day broke. After a brief reconnaissance, they discovered that the Indians were sleeping in apparent security and that their horses, about five hundred in number, were grazing near the village. Young Ross with his Indian scouts soon rounded up the horses and drifted them out of the reach of the Comanches, forcing them to fight on foot.

According to Wilbarger's as well as Ross' account, just at sunrise Major Van Dorn, with a number of soldiers, charge the upper end of the village while Captain Ross, with the remaining soldiers and Indian scouts, charged the lower end. The village was strung along the banks of a branch or creek for a distance of three or four hundred yards. The morning was very foggy and, after the battle was begun, it was difficult to distinguish one object from another. The Comanches fought with perfect desperation, as their women and children were in peril. A few moments after the engagement began in earnest, Captain Ross saw a number of Indians running down the creek, about one hundred and fifty yards from the village. Ross and his Caddo Indian scout pursued them, and found that they were women and children. Soon another fleeing posse came along, among whom was a little white girl. Ross ordered his Caddo scout to catch her but the girl, finding herself in the hands of a strange Indian, was very hard to control. The Caddo eventually succeeded in securing her.

Ross soon discovered that twenty-five or thirty warriors stood between himself and Major Van Dorn, and were rushing upon him allowing no chance for escape. Lieutenants Van Camp and Alexander were killed before they could fire upon the enemy. Ross attempted to fire but his rifle snapped. Mohee, a Comanche warrior, seized Alexander's gun, shot and wounded Ross who fell upon his pistol. Mohee was advancing upon him, knife in hand, evidently intending to kill and scalp him, when the signal for retreat was given by the Comanches. Mohee turned and ran. As he ran, Lieutenant Majors shot him in the back and he fell dead. Ross knew Mohee well, having seen him often at the Indian agency, and recognized him immediately.

The faithful Caddo succeeded in safely holding the little white girl whom he had captured. Through the terrible battle they both passed, neither of them hurt in the least. The whole battle consumed only a few minutes and, while Captain Evans held the lower end of the village and Major Van Dorn held the upper end, the Comanches escaped to the hills.

The brave Van Dorn received an arrow wound. When he fell, it was thought that he was mortally wounded. On account of the severity of their wounds, the two leaders, Ross and Van Dorn, had to remain on the battlefield for several days. They were carried toward Fort Belknap upon litters by the friendly Indian scouts. Upon reaching Camp Radziminski, they obtained an ambulance, which rendered the remainder of their journey much more comfortable. Major Van Dorn soon recovered and made another successful raid. After his recovery, Sul Ross returned to the military school in Alabama where he completed his course in college and graduated in 1859.

This skirmish was known as the Battle of the Wichita Mountains. The Comanches lost about ninety killed and many more wounded, in addition to all of their camp equipage, supplies and horses. The loss to the white men was but five men killed.

After arriving at the settlements and forming acquaintances among the white people, the little white girl captive formed an ardent friendship with Miss Lizzie Tinsley, who went on to marry General Sul Ross. In honor of the former Miss Tinsley, the young captive girl took the name Lizzie Ross. She became an accomplished and well educated lady and, while on a visit with General Ross' mother to California, she was married to a wealthy merchant and is still making her home in her adopted state. Every possible means was exhausted in search for the parents or former friends of Lizzie Ross, but at last the conclusion was drawn that they had all been killed at the time of the massacre during which Lizzie was taken captive.

Battle of Pease River &
Recapture of Cynthia Ann Parker

After reading Wilbarger's *Indian Depredations in Texas*, many of the nearly forgotten incidents of the past have been revived in my memory. I was present on the frontier at the time many of the events occurred, and knew well the particulars as related by Wilbarger. I vividly remember when Cynthia Ann Parker was captured. I was well acquainted with her uncle, Isaac D. Parker, and knew several of the rangers who were with General Ross at the time of her capture. I have read a number of accounts, given by others, of her capture but I believe the one given by Wilbarger is by far the most accurate. Judge Z. E. Coombes, a brother-in-law of mine with whom I was very close, was a teacher in the Indian school at the old Brazos agency at the time S. P. Ross was the agent, and was very intimate with him. Though I was much younger than Judge Coombes, I knew very well about Ross, Major Neighbors and others at the agency. They are all, I suppose, dead, as I am in my sixty-fifth year.

For years after the great defeat at the Battle of Wichita Mountains, the Comanches were much less troublesome and made but a few raids into the settlements. In 1859, they again began raiding and became much worse than they'd been before. They were soon so troublesome that the people were forced to be well armed at all times. Even the workmen in the fields did not feel safe unless they had their guns within reach and ready for use upon short notice. The raids became more troublesome because the Comanches were well acquainted with the country in which they were raiding, having once occupied it as their home or hunting ground. I prefer to refer to it as a hunting ground, as the Comanches and Kiowas seemed not to have any fixed home, but were rambling tribes, often crossing the Plains into the Rocky Mountains. They generally kept their families in the breaks at the eastern edge of the Staked Plains, where they were in reach of the settlements upon which they could make their raids. No doubt they not only raided for purposes of plunder, but also hoped thereby to prevent the rapid encroachment of the white man upon that which they considered to be Indian country.

After the removal of the Indian agency from Fort Belknap across the Red River to Fort Sill in 1860, at the beginning of the Civil War, both life and property were extremely unsafe on the frontier. Just at this time, Peta Nocona—chief of the Comanches, husband of the lamented Cynthia Ann Parker and father of the present Comanche chief, Quanah Parker—made a sweeping raid through the counties of Young, Jack and Parker. It will not be out of place here, I hope, to mention that Parker County was named for Isaac D. Parker, an uncle of Cynthia Ann. The noted Peta Nocona on this raid displayed his thorough knowledge of the country by the rapidity through which he passed through it, and his successful escape when pursued. Had he lived to continue these raids during the Civil War, when both men and arms were so scarce, it is difficult to conceive what would have been the consequence to the frontier counties. This emphasizes the great credit due to General Sul Ross for defeating him in the battle to be described here.

For some time after Peta Nocona had made the raids through the counties above mentioned, on which he killed the Younglboods, the Rippys and many others, on moonlit nights the people of the settlements were in perfect dread, and ever on watch, listening even to the hooting of an owl or the howl of the wolves, fearing that those sounds were only imitations made by the Comanches as signals. I remember well the time when the beautiful nights of the full moon, instead of being a source of pleasure were, on the contrary, dreaded as the worst of evils. I learned to dread a bright night so much that, for years afterwards, I could not enjoy them as I do now. Even at this date, such nights awaken within me sad thoughts of the past that are anything but pleasant.

To hasten an end to this dread, an effective appeal was made by the settlers to the government for protection and

Colonel M. T. Johnson was authorized to raise a regiment for the purpose of repressing Indian depredations. During one expedition, Col. Johnson's command made a signal failure and the wily Comanches, eluding him at every point, followed him closely upon his return and captured a great many of his horses and mules before he reached the settlements. This cast a feeling of gloom and uneasiness over the entire west.

After Captain Sul Ross returned from school in Alabama, he was commissioned by Governor Houston and, with a company of sixty men, he went to Fort Belknap and received the same equipage that had been used by Colonel Johnson. Calling upon the commander at Fort Cooper, Captain N. G. Evans, for help, Ross was reinforced by a squad of twenty other men, giving him a total of eighty in all. Captain Evans and his men had been with Ross on a former expedition and they each had gained the mutual confidence of the other. The settlers, in addition, volunteered to the cause seventy men under the command of Captain Jack Cureton of Bosque County, swelling the number of men to about one hundred and fifty. After supplying the command with a large number of pack mules, well laden with such things as they would need, they proceeded on an expedition into Nocona's own country. I give below the details of their work as given by Captain Ross himself, as found in Wilbarger's history:

"On the 18th of December, 1860, while marching up the Pease River, I had suspicions that Indians were in the vicinity, by reason of the buffalo that came running in great numbers from the north toward us. While my command moved in the low ground, I visited all neighboring high points to make discoveries. On one of these sand hills, I found four fresh pony tracks and, being satisfied that Indian vedettes had just gone, I galloped forward about a mile to a higher point and, on reaching the top, to my inexpressible surprise, I found myself within two hundred yards of a Comanche village located on a small stream winding around the base of the hill. It was a happy circumstance that a piercing north wind was blowing, carrying the sound with it and my presence was wholly unobserved and was a complete surprise. I signalled my men and they reached me without being discovered by the Indians, who were busy packing up preparatory to a move. By this time, the Indians mounted and moved off north, across a level plain. My command, with a detachment of the Second Cavalry, had outmarched and become separated from the citizen command, leaving me with about sixty men.

"In making disposition for the attack, the sergeant and his twenty men were sent at a gallop behind a chain of sand hills, to encompass the Indians and cut off their retreat, while with forty men I charged. The attack was so sudden that quite a number were killed before they could prepare for defense. They fled precipitately, right into the presence of the sergeant and his men. Here they met with a warm reception and, finding themselves completely encompassed, each fled his own way and was hotly pursued and hard pressed. The chief of the party was Peta Nocona, a noted warrior of great repute, with a young girl about fifteen years of age mounted behind him. Cynthia Ann Parker, with a girl about two years old in her arms, mounted on a fleet pony, fled together with the chief while Lieutenant Kellihier and I pursued them. After running about a mile, Kellihier rode up by the side of Cynthia's horse and, as I was in the act of shooting, she held up her child and stopped. I kept on after the chief and in about a half a mile I fired my pistol, striking the girl (whom I supposed was a man, as she rode like one, and only her head was visible above the buffalo robe in which she was wrapped) near the heart and killed her instantly. The same ball would have killed both, but for the shield of the chief which hung down, covering his back.

"When the girl fell from the horse, she pulled the chief off also, but he caught on his feet and, before he could steady himself, my horse, running at full speed, was very nearly on top of him. At this time, my horse was struck with an arrow which caused him to begin pitching or bucking and it was with great difficulty that I kept my saddle and, in the meantime, narrowly escaped several arrows coming in quick succession from the chief's bow. As I had such a disadvantage, the chief would have killed me but for a random shot from my pistol (fired while I was clinging with my left hand to the pommel of my saddle) which broke his right arm at the elbow, completely disabling him. My horse then became quiet and I shot the chief twice through the body, whereupon he deliberately walked to a small tree—the only one in sight—and, leaning against it, began to sing a wild, weird song.

"At this time, my Mexican servant, who had once been a captive with the Comanches and spoke their language fluently, came up in company with two of my men. I then summoned the chief to surrender, but he promptly treated every overture with contempt, and signified his declaration with a savage attempt to thrust me with the lance that he held in his left hand. I could only look upon him with pity and admiration. For, deplorable as was his situation—with no chance of escape, his party utterly destroyed, his wife and child captured in his sight—he was undaunted by the fate that awaited him. And he seemed to prefer death to life. I directed the Mexican to end his misery with a charge of buckshot from the gun he carried.

"Taking up the chief's accoutrements, which I later sent to Governor Houston to be placed in the archives at Austin, we rode back to Cynthia Ann Parker and Kellihier. I found the latter belittling himself for running his pet horse so hard after an old squaw. As soon as I looked at her face, I said, 'Why, Tom, this is a white woman. Indians don't have blue eyes.' On the way to where my men were assembling with the spoils and a large collection of Indian horses, I discovered an Indian boy about nine years old, secreted in the grass. Expecting to be killed, he began to cry but I made him mount behind me on my horse. In later years, I frequently proposed to send him back to his people, but he steadily refused to go. He died in McLennan County last year.

"After we camped for the night, Cynthia Ann continued crying and we felt the cause was her fear of death. I had the Mexican tell her that we recognized her as one of our own people and would not harm her. She said that two of her boys were with her when the fight began and that she was distressed by fear that they were killed. It so happened that they both escaped unharmed and one of them, Quanah, is now a great chief. The other died some years ago on the plains. I then asked her to give me a history of her life with the Indians and the circumstances attending her capture, which she promptly did in a very sensible manner. As the facts detailed corresponded with the massacre at Parker's Fort, I was impressed with the belief that she was, in fact, Cynthia Ann Parker.

"When I returned to my post, I sent her and her child to the ladies at Cooper where she could secure the attention that her situation demanded and, at the same time, dispatched a messenger to her uncle, Colonel Parker, near Weatherford. Since I was called to Waco to meet Governor Houston, I left directions for the Mexican to accompany Colonel Parker to Cooper in the capacity of an interpreter. When Colonel Parker reached that place, her identity was confirmed, to his entire satisfaction and great happiness."

Thus was fought the great battle of Pease River, with the great Comanche chief, Peta Nocona with a strong force on one side, and the brave Captain Ross with sixty Rangers on the other. In the fight, the greater part of the warriors were killed and such a victory had never before been gained over these Comanches. This battle did more for the protection of our frontier during the war than almost everything else combined.

Cynthia Ann Parker, who was captured at the massacre at Parker's Fort in 1836 and was with the Comanches for twenty-five years, was recaptured by the gallant Captain Ross who at once arranged for her uncle, Isaac D. Parker, to meet her with an interpreter at Camp Cooper. When Colonel Parker saw her, he said, "My niece's name was Cynthia Ann." Upon hearing her name, her face lit up with a smile, which it had not done since her capture by Ross on Pease River and, patting herself on the breast she said, "Me Cynthia Ann; me Cynthia Ann." Her uncle was greatly delighted at the evidence of her identity, which was beyond question. She was really Cynthia Ann Parker but, oh, how she'd changed! Although she was all sunburnt and brown, with almost a savage expression fixed upon her face, her uncle was nearly overjoyed that their own Cynthia Ann was back again with those who loved her and had for so long mourned her as dead. Her friends all welcomed her back with great joy and did all in their power to render her happy and to make her feel at home with them, but it was with considerable difficulty that she was restrained from returning in search of her boys, from whom she had been as ruthlessly torn as she had been from her parents at the massacre at Parker's Fort.

Gradually her native language returned to her and she was able to recall many of the scenes of her childhood and remember some friends of her family, among whom was the aged Father Anglin. She soon learned to discharge the domestic duties in good order but never for a moment did she forget her boys. She wished to see them and she ardently hoped that, when the war should close, she would be able to meet them again. This pleasure was not for her, however, for ere the white-winged angel of peace had hovered over our land, her little daughter, Prairie Flower, who was with her at the time of her recapture, passed from earth to that home above, and Cynthia Ann soon followed.

Thus ends the story of the well-known woman talked about so much throughout our frontier for the last forty years. Before closing the history of the Parkers, we must make brief mention of her boys, who were so suddenly deprived of both parents and left orphans with their tribe at the battle of Pease River. The details we have concerning their lives after the battle are meager, but it is known that they accompanied their red friends across the staked plains into the Rocky Mountains. This must have been a very trying ordeal to them. Not only had they been deprived of the protecting care of their parents—their father killed and their mother made a captive by the hated white man from whom they expected that she would receive nothing else but cruelty and death—but a severe winter was raging and the tribe had lost all their winter supplies and entire equipage. They had to cross the Great American Desert in the dead of winter with none of the comforts of even savage life, perhaps on foot and through the snow and blizzards of that bare plain.

One of the boys died on those dreary plains a number of years after the recapture of their mother. The other, Captain Quanah, owns in his own right a fine ranch, lives in a fine, well-furnished house and has about him the comforts usually found in a civilized and refined home. He still fondly cherishes the memory of his beloved mother. After being placed on the reservation, he sought her picture and, when it was obtained, he recognized her features and exclaimed "Prelock! Prelock!" (her Indian name) and was overjoyed to have possession of the photograph. He certainly exhibited great affection for his mother and, by the close guardianship which he has exercised over his tribe as their chief and his devotion to their every interest, he has shown a degree of unselfishness and intelligence not to be expected from one of the Indian race.

ELDRIDGE PEACE COMMISSION

While there have been a number of histories written by different parties giving general accounts of the Indians on the Southwestern frontier, none of them give detailed accounts of many of the thrilling incidents which occurred from 1850 to 1876, when the Indian were subdued and placed on the Reservation.

John Henry Brown wrote one of the most thorough accounts ever given of the Indians on the Southwestern frontier and his history of Texas, in two volumes, is the most complete one ever written. He gives an account of the Indians from the earliest settlement in Texas and shows how many tribes of Indians have now become extinct. Quite a number of them, in order to get between the two armies—the Mexican on one side and the American on the other—moved, either across the Rio Grande into Mexico or across the Red River into what is now Indian Territory. There were still quite a number who lived back more toward the plains and consequently were not brought so much in contact with the armies and settlements until after the Mexican War.

When the settlements began reaching West toward the plains, the settlement of this country soon brought up more friction. There were then quite a number of fragmentary tribes having, it seemed, no particular place of abode. Sam Houston, who was President of the Republic, now in its greatest struggle for independence, was unable to meet the great emergencies for the frontier's protection and at the same time stand in readiness for the great conflict with Mexico yet to come, on which the lives, liberties and property rights of the people were dependent.

During the cessation of hostilities which came about in 1843, in which General Santa Anna sought to make terms with Texas whereby it would become a part of Mexico, it was readily observed that this armistice could only last a short time. Texas would again be plunged into war and would be in need of all available men and means. General

Houston, desiring to avoid bloodshed, attempted to secure a permanent treaty of peace with all of the wild tribes. In order to accomplish this, he sent Joe C. Eldridge as an ambassador to visit them and to induce them to attend a peace council to be held near where the city of Waco is now situated.

Eldridge took with him two tried and true friends, H. P. Bee (General Bee) and Thomas Torrey, a truly brave man. He also had with him several Delaware Indians and the head chief of the Wacos, who proved not only a true friend but one of the bravest of men. Thus equipped, Eldridge left from the town of Washington, then capital of Texas, on one of the most perilous expeditions of which I have ever read. It may be that a person who has had the misfortune to pass through such a trying ordeal can more readily appreciate the situation and what it means to have life suspended upon so brittle a thread with no room for hope and then, at the critical moment, have the balance turn in his favor and his liberty, and almost his life, restored.

It seemed that Eldridge and his co-ambassadors, Bee and Torrey, were so completely committed to their tasks that the thought of danger never entered their minds until they were brought face to face with death. They journeyed with no means of protection but their own strong arms and brave hearts, and the strong ties of friendship of the great Waco chief, Acoquash. This chief was truly a great man of heroic valor in the time of trial, with a high sense of honor, and true and abiding loyalty.

While they were to visit all of the wild tribes on their way, their main object was to enlist the fiercest ad the wildest of all the Western Indians—the Comanches and the Kiowas. They crossed the Brazos River below where Waco is now situated and, there, met some of the Tehuacanos. From there, they proceeded to where the city of Dallas is now situated. Here they met other tribes. Upon reaching the cross timbers, perhaps where Wise County is now located, they met quite a number, among whom were some opposed to their scheme of peacemaking but, undaunted, the party

moved on in a northwesterly direction, crossing the Red
River. Traveling along the north bank of that stream, they
came upon the camp of one of the most powerful of the
Indian tribes—the Wichitas. The Indians, it seemed, were
willing to go into the peace conference.

Our party marched west from this camp into what is now
known as the Panhandle. One day, as they approached a
small stream, they found that someone had been gathering and eating plums. Presently an old Indian with a boy,
mounted on his horse in front of him, approached. They
found that he was an old chief and that he was blind.
The boy was his guide and had been instructed to gather
plums. When the chief had all the plums he wanted, he
conducted Eldridge and his party to his camp. There, they
learned that he was head chief of the Comanches. They
obtained directions to the Comanche camp and when
they reached it, they were kindly received by the wife of
Pahayuco, the blind Comanche head chief. She arranged a
tent for them and there they waited a week for Pahayuco's
return. During this time they were treated well, except
that the Indians, especially the younger ones, thronged
about them continually, never having seen white men before. These young Indians would come and peep into their
sleeves or roll them up to see their white skin.

Finally, one evening, Pahayuco came and kindly received
Eldridge and his men. The next morning, their mission
was made known and Pahayuco called a council of one
hundred of his warriors and chiefs. Eldridge and his white
companions were not invited to this council, which caused
them some apprehension of danger. The Indians who had
accompanied Eldridge participated in the council, among
whom was the noble Acoquash, the Waco chief. After some
deliberation by the council, the Delaware Jim Shaw returned to Eldridge and informed him that everything was
alright. This did not satisfy them, however, for they had
heard every speech delivered to the council and had noticed the manner of speaking, as well as other proceedings
of the council which indicated great dissatisfaction among

the Indians. This caused great alarm among Eldridge and his men.

Presently, Acoquash came trembling with great fear and with tears rolling down his cheeks. Kneeling by Eldridge, he said that the Indians were going to put them to death and that he intended to die with them. He had told the council that they had come to make peace, and that they carried the pretty white flag of peace with them. He told them that if they killed his white friends, the Great Spirit would not be good to them; that he was the son of a great Waco chief who had always given them good advice; that he was old and they should listen to him, for he, too, would give them good advice. Acoquash said that they shook their heads and would not hear him. He said that he would go back to the council and try again and if they would not hear him, he would return and die with his white friends.

When Acoquash had gone, Jim Shaw came again. Eldridge asked him why he had tried to deceive them, and Shaw replied that he dared not let them know the truth because it was so bad. "It is true," he said. "They are going to kill you, but Pahayuco is yet to speak." This was in the afternoon and it seemed that each member of the council had spoken but the chief. It was late before he spoke and when he did, he told the council that these men bore the white flag and came on a mission of peace, and that if they killed the white men, the Great Spirit would not be good to them. During his discourse, some of the Delawares came and informed Eldridge that Pahayuco was favorable to them, but that the warriors just shook their heads.

Just as the sun was going down that evening, Bee said to his companions, "Look at the sun setting, for we will never see that sight again." The party had agreed, when notified of their awful danger, that when the Indians should come to take them out for death, each would kill an Indian with one of his pistols and then, to escape the slow inevitable torture, empty the other pistol into his own brain.

Finally, the old chief took the vote. When it was counted, old Acoquash came rushing into the tent and grabbed up Eldridge in his arms. He was too excited to speak and seemed completely overcome. When he had sufficiently recovered, he said that all was right, that the vote had been taken and was in their favor, exclaiming, "We are safe! We are safe!" Eldridge and his men bowed in reverence to the Giver of every good and perfect gift, and lifted their voices in thanksgiving to Him for their wonderful deliverance. Years afterward, General Bee said that words were inadequate to describe the scene or their expressions of joy and gratitude—the red man and the white man in fond embrace, weeping for joy and the good old Acoquash more joyous than them all. Occasionally such instances came up in dealing with the Indian that would justify the expression "the noble red man." This was one of those instances.

After the council adjourned, the Eldridge party heard Pahayuco in loud tones commanding his men. He encircled the tent of the white men with a strong guard, instructing them to let no one enter that circle, and that he who harmed the white men would die. When they had been assured of their safety, they took a quiet night's rest and arose the next morning to see the sun rise with almost renewed splendor and beauty, bringing another day of real joy.

Before leaving the Comanche camp, Captain Eldridge tendered to the chief little Maria, a beautiful Indian child neatly dressed, who knew no tongue but English, and a little Comanche boy who had taken the name of William Hockley, both of whom had been captured in the Council House Fight at San Antonio. A scene followed which brought tears to the eyes of not only the white men but also the red. The girl seemed horrified and, clinging desperately and imploringly to Captain Eldridge, screamed piteously. She was taken by a huge warrior and borne away. For years afterward, she acted as interpreter at Indian councils. The boy remembered his mother tongue and soon relapsed into savagery.

By the time Eldridge returned to President Houston, so much time had been lost on the expedition that the President had despaired of their return, had left the place of meeting and returned to the place of government. The commissioners who remained at the council in Waco had made an agreement with quite a number of the tribes dwelling nearest the settlements. This gave a degree of protection to the whites and prevented any annoyance for several years.

The kindly feeling between the Indians and the whites lasted for a number of years after the annexation of Texas. I think great credit is due to Sam Houston, Bee, Eldridge and others for their good example and for bringing concil-iatory influence to bear upon them. As I have stated, many tribes of Indians had either removed to Mexico or the Indian Territory, and many who remained seemed to retain peaceful sentiments. The change that came over the country was so great after annexation that the whites, as well as the Indians, hardly realized that the powerful arm of the United States was now to protect as well as to control.

TREATMENT OF THE INDIANS
BY THE U. S. GOVERNMENT

Much of what follows is drawn from my own personal observation. I will first relate the conditions that existed on the frontier with regard to the means of protection used by the United States government, the treatment given to the Indians and the methods used in controlling them. I do this in order to present some of the leading characteristics of the Indians and to show the cause of our Indian troubles. These troubles should not be charged to the Indians alone, nor attributed to the policy of the government in general. They were, however, partly due to the rash and unwise conduct of some of the government officers.

At this time, there was a line of forts from the Red River to the Rio Grande, of which Fort Worth and Fort Graham are two. A plain road ran from one post to another. Up to about 1852, the Indians were permitted to come in and hunt game east of this road and line of forts. When they were around the settlement, they appeared very friendly, visited our homes and gave us wild game. They had a way of skinning deer, leaving the hide nearly whole, and afterwards sewing up the openings. When the hide was well dried in this shape, they often filled it with honey from bee trees found in the woods. Sometimes they would divide the honey with us, but they annoyed us greatly by begging coffee and tobacco. Of course, they would steal it if they had a suitable opportunity.

They would sometimes steal horses, but never when they were on a friendly visit. If no Indians were seen for a spell, however, it was often said, "We had better look out for our horses." When they did steal horses and the old settlers could get started on their trail in time, five or six men could take a bunch of horses from a hundred Indians. Our people had rifles while they only had bows and arrows.

In 1852, the officer in command at Fort Worth issued an order for the Indians to stay west of the road. Shortly afterward, a hunting party of Indians came over into the cross timbers and camped near where the town of Mansfield is now situated. They ranged out into Mountain Creek valley, near where I lived, killing game but disturbing no one. A scout of soldiers was sent out from Fort Worth to put them back across the line. They arrested many Indians and whipped many across their naked backs, threatening to kill them if they were found across the line again.

There was one young Indian, seventeen or eighteen years of age, who had been separated from his people when they were arrested and taken away. Knowing not what had become of them, he returned to their camp. He began a search but the trail had been beaten out by the soldiers' horses, as the Indians had been kept in front and the soldiers followed behind them on horseback. This young Indian made a circle of the country on a hunt for the trail of his people. During this trek, he met some of our settlers who told him what had happened. This was fortunate for us, for it allowed us to locate the blame for the harsh treatment where it properly belonged. I shall never forget that young Indian's distress in his search. He would travel some distance, give his Indian whoop and wait for a reply, but none came. When he was informed of what had happened, he made directly for the west and, I suppose, he then knew where to go as I never heard of him afterward.

The Indians were here first and were forced out of a country they regarded as their own by our superior strength and equipments. I do not want to be understood as justifying these cruel, bloody-handed people, but wish to show them in their true light—a degraded, ignorant wicked people whose destiny time and eternity alone will reveal.

One of the peculiarities of the Indians was their jealousy of any infringement of their rights, and their hatred of those who disturbed their tranquility or encroached upon their possessions by means of superior strength. While they were kind and true to friends, they were cruel and merciless to their enemies or opponents. When the young Indian was told of the fate of his people, he certainly remembered the kindness, for that neighborhood was never afterwards disturbed by the Indians.

There were a great many very bad men who were renegades from the Old States and fugitives from justice who came into this new country. They depredated both on the whites and the Indians, but stayed principally out beyond the settlements. One particular group of such fellows robbed the camps belonging to friendly Indians and killed two of the Indians. In order to create excitement and make their escape, they came into the settlement and reported that Indians were coming down the West Fork of the Trinity, killing everyone they encountered. The alarm went out all along the frontier and the people were notified to assemble at Waxahachie to prepare for defense.

Though the report of Indians was false, it had the same effect as if it were true. The evident object of the robbers was to get up a scare. The report aroused the whole country, reaching our house around nightfall. Nearly everyone got up teams and horses, and made the drive to Waxahachie only to learn upon their arrival that the statements were false. For some reason, my father did not believe the story. However, he arranged the next morning for the family to go. When we had gone about half way, perhaps seven or eight miles from home, we met people returning who informed us that the reports were false. My father did not accompany us, but went off in another direction to investigate the truthfulness of what we had heard. On our return home that evening, we had a great many jokes on one another about getting scared over nothing.

The whole scare was a great deal like the fable of the fox and the grapes. A farmer hung a large bell in his grapevine to frighten the fox that was coveting his grapes. The fox came, and when he began to climb the vine, the bell rattled. He jumped down and fled. He returned again to investigate the cause of his fright and, as he climbed up and caused the bell to rattle, instead of running away as formerly, he would stop, wait awhile and listen. In this way, he finally reached the bell. After inspecting it closely, he said, "You great big hollow-headed thing, how you scared me!"

After this Indian scare, like the fox, we waited before we ran. It was not long until, one bright pretty day, some member of the family looked out across the rolling hills to the west and saw an old buffalo running from some fright in full view of our house. Immediately followed what appeared to be forty or fifty men on horseback—but they suddenly stopped. We watched in great earnestness as they stood perfectly still more than a mile away, and looked like so many Indians ready to make a charge upon our home at any moment. They were but mustangs. After this bunch of mustang horses stood still, with high arched necks, viewing the surroundings for a time, they, like the buffalo, galloped away.

Nothing in those days escaped our notice, nor the vigilance of our watchful eyes. Scenes of this kind were of frequent occurrence, but the posture of these mustangs gave them the real appearance of mounted horsemen, and the excitement of the Indian scare just preceding blended imagination with the scene. The Indian summer weather with its smoky, hazy appearance added to the impression an unusual apprehension. The stimulating effect of the excitement, especially when not accompanied with true danger, seems to drive away dull care, to enliven the action of the mind, to invite new thoughts and to give a new flavor to life. It had a social effect as well, if the excitement was such as to bring the people together to talk it over.

The excitement of our Indian scare was kept alive in our neighborhood by the neighbors meeting together and relating the many funny incidents connected with it. One of our neighbors told this amusing tale on himself. While they were preparing for the trip to Waxahachie that night, he missed one of his shoes. The rest of the family was ready to go, but he kept searching for his shoe. They said, "You will stay here looking for that shoe until we all lose our scalps!" He replied to this by saying, "How do you expect me to run fast enough to save my scalp with only one shoe?!" This man, Uncle Billy Bradford, was a cripple and couldn't run at all. I knew him long after to be in some Indian excitements not so funny.

When Indian affairs, as well as the protection of the settlers, was placed in the hands of the government, arrangements were commenced to place the Indians on reservations. Two agents were appointed. One was S. P. Ross, who acted as local agent in receiving and disbursing supplies and who had charge of all dealings with the Indians. The other, General Neighbors, was the general agent for all the Indians. Somehow people were not pleased with the latter because of his influence and the influence of the desperate characters lodged along the frontier. This, together with some further Indian depredations, built up a prejudice against the agents as well as the agencies, but it did not seem to be directed against Ross so much as it was Neighbors.

Wherever the blame is to be laid, the effort to peacefully handle Indians was proving fruitless, so far as Texas was concerned. There were two reservations arranged on the Brazos River—one below Fort Belknap, the other above it. The former was occupied by several small tribes and parts of tribes, the latter by Comanches and Kiowas. The people had become so dissatisfied that they went out under the command of Colonel John Baylor to break up the agency by force. On arriving at the reservation, they declined to make an attack, as it would seem more against the U.S. troops than against the Indians, and they abandoned the project.

The hostile feelings against the Indians, however, were so intense that Governor Hardin, Sam Houston and R. Runnels sought to have the Indians removed across the Red River. The removal actually occurred in 1860, and although it was done quietly without any exhibition of hostility further than that of Baylor and his men, it produced considerable angst among the Indians. When the Civil War came up, all the troops were removed and the country was stripped of arms by the enlistment of our men in the Confederate Army. The whole frontier was without any means of protection other than that afforded by the stockmen and their hands on the range. Cattle had multiplied so rapidly that ranches were established all along the frontier, standing like so many forts, and serving as a means of protection and place of resort when the Indians made their raids.

MURDER OF THE BABB FAMILY

Around some of the ranches that sprang up during the Civil War occurred some of the most terrible and atrocious Indian massacres of record. John Babb had a ranch in Wise County, twelve or fourteen miles west of the county seat of Decatur. He lived in a place remote from the settlement, near a frequented pass of the Indians, and one day left his family alone without any means of protection. Mrs. Babb had a baby just old enough to sit up on its own, a little girl some larger, a boy named Dott who was eight or nine years of age and a girl twelve or thirteen years old. With them lived a beautiful young widow who, I presume, acted as a governess.

During the absence of Mr. Babb, Colonel Pickett of Decatur passed the ranch and, for some reason, had a presentiment that something was wrong. So deep was this feeling that he turned around and rode to the ranch house. In a report afterwards made by him to a reporter of the *Dallas News*, Colonel Pickett said, in substance:

"As I approached the house, the impression seemed to grow stronger. When I reached the fence and found it torn down, I was in a tremor of excitement. I ran to the house and pushed open the door. The first thing I beheld was the baby's face as it peeped over it's mother's bloody bosom to look at me. Its face was covered with blood from its mother's breast, where it had evidently been trying to obtain nourishment. The mother had been shot down with the babe in her arms and had fallen with it across the bed, where the child had remained all this time without attention and was almost perishing for something to eat.

"In the backyard, two of the children had been killed. A boy, a girl and the widow governess had been carried away captive by the Indians. The beauty of the young woman had, no doubt, saved her life. At the massacre, the Indians had stolen one of Babb's fine race horses, and upon him the widow was placed and led away to the Indian Territory. Twenty miles beyond the Red River, they stopped and arrangements were made for this accomplished young woman to marry their chief two moons later. They placed her in the charge of an old squaw, to be kept during that period. Under this guard, she was separated from the main camp.

One night, when the moon was full orbed to shine all night with no clouds to obscure its brilliance, the widow saw that Babb's fine race stallion had been staked out near her tent. When the old squaw was sound asleep, the young woman slipped away to the horse and, placing a rope around his nose for a bridle, sprang astride his back and galloped away unobserved. After a twenty mile ride, she reached the Red River and, to her dismay, observed that its waters were very high. By the light of the moon, she could see the drift logs and trash rolling downstream and, with fear, gazed upon the turbulent waters. The horse pressed forward, impatient for being held in check and desirous, it seemed, of crossing over to the other side. The widow contemplated death as the most probable result if she undertook the task, but remembered that hesitation meant a fate worse than death, for she would be compelled to marry that dusky demon.

The reins slackened and into the river plunged horse and rider. Time passed slowly to her as the waters rolled and tumbled round about, and the fast drifting logs passed on either side. But the horse was one of great power and nerve and finally reached the other bank in safety. Rising on the Texas side, from what had seemed like a certain watery grave, they were safe from the hand of a cruel foe. Out they sped through the river bottom and up across the hills to a large prairie. Fatigued by the ride and the excitement of the journey, she stopped her noble horse, tied him to a small tree and laid down to take a much needed rest just as the day was beginning to dawn.

Near midday, she was awakened by the tramping of hooves and, springing up, found herself surrounded by another band of Indians. Her flight had ended in a second capture—this time by the Comanches. They placed

her again on a horse and took her far away from the settlements near the head of the Red River to their Indian
village. Again she was doomed to marry a chief and again
was placed in the hands of an old squaw. But the marriage,
this time, was to be three moons away. A cultured and refined woman was sentenced yet again to marry a savage.
She was a remarkable woman who, though far away from
her Texas home and friends, never lost hope nor courage,
no matter how unbearable her captivity.

Her opportunity to escape at last came. Again at night,
on the same horse, she made her escape and, to elude her
cruel masters, she galloped away in the opposite direction
of her home. She was more fortunate this time and found
the trail of a wagon train the next day, which she followed
rapidly, at last overtaking a train of freight wagons. With
these freighters, the widow journeyed to Fort Supply,
where she became acquainted with a Kansas family whom
she accompanied to their home in Kansas. She was afterward married to a prosperous stockman and raised a large
family. She still lives, loved and respected by a large circle
of friends. She knew nothing of what became of the Babb
children after they reached the first Indian camp.

The children were recovered from captivity by purchase
at a price of forty saddle horses. In this connection, I wish
to give credit to the negro, Brit, who in an effort to recover
his own wife and two children from the Comanches, was
instrumental in arranging for the purchase of the Babb
children. The children were brought back to their home in
Wise County where they were reared and educated. Dott
Babb has been sheriff of Wichita County and now resides
there, a respected and honored citizen. His sister resides
in Henrietta, Texas, an accomplished and refined lady.

The Elm Creek Raid of 1864

As stated in another place in this book, it seems that many of the most thrilling events that took place during the dark days of our Indian troubles were viewed by different people in different ways. Perhaps it is a fault of memory which causes the accounts given by different people to vary so widely. It is impossible now, in giving a history of so fearful a raid as that made on Elm Creek in Young County, to present an exact statement of the events as they actually transpired. I have recently read the account furnished in the *Dallas News* by Mr. J. W. Proffit of Young County and have conversed with Mr. T. K. Hamby of Baylor County— both were participants in the struggle. These sources will cause our telling of the story to have a slight variance from accounts that have been recently published. As further testimony to the accuracy of these sources, I will further state that the writer was, at the time of the raid, not far away. I moved into the community soon after the raid and received from numerous participants, first hand, these facts. So I can, without a doubt, vouch for their accuracy.

During a period when nearly all men were absent on a cattle drive, drifting their stock back on the range, and the women and children were almost without protection, this raid was made. An unusually large body of Comanche Indians came down the Brazos River on the north side. They crossed near the mouth of Elm Creek. Their first depredation was at Mose Johnson's ranch. There, they murdered Mrs. Deargan and a child of the family of a negro named Brit who belonged to Johnson. They scalped Mrs. Deargan but did not scalp the negro child. They carried off old lady Patrick and two of her granddaughters (children of Mrs. Johnson) and negro Brit's wife and two of their children, as captives. It is appropriate here to illustrate a specific characteristic of the Comanche Indian. Old lady Patrick displayed great weakness and was almost overcome with fright, while Brit's wife was independent and self-reliant, resenting every insult and cruelty. If they came about her or her children, she would attack them with a stick or any available weapon. Brit's wife was appreciated by the Indians for her lack of fear, while Mrs. Patrick was cruelly treated on account of her timidity.

The raiders then moved up Elm Creek, capturing each of the ranches as they came to them. Before the Indians reached Hamby's ranch, the elder Hamby, Dr. Wilson and Thornt Hamby had conveyed the women and children from the ranch and concealed themselves under some shelving rocks. In this manner, they saved their own lives and proceeded in advance of the Indians giving the alarm. This notice, no doubt, saved a number of lives.

The Comanches captured and destroyed the ranches of the Spranges and Uncle Harry Williams. At the latter place, the families were concealed in the same manner as at Hamby's. Jim Williams, a son of Uncle Harry, who resides at present at the town of Benjamin, was a small boy at the time of the raid. He says he wanted terribly for water while in hiding, but fear of the Indians kept him from crying. The Hambys, Dr. Wilson and other men reached Bragg's Fort. The Indians were in close pursuit.

The men entered the fort and prepared for defense as well and as quickly as possible. There were quite a number of women and children in the fort. George Bragg, a negro boy eighteen or twenty years of age, and the men previously mentioned, constituted the fighting force. The negro boy did the loading. The fort was so constructed that there was but one opening through which the Indians could have forced an entrance. At this place Thornt Hamby, who had just returned from the Confederate army, was stationed. He had brought home with him a repeating rifle. He was also armed with a double-barrel shotgun.

Just as the men had completed their preparations, the Indians surrounded the little fort and, with their hideous yells, commenced their charge. There were port holes and cracks in the walls. Soon after the little battle began, Dr. Wilson was killed and George Bragg was wounded. The savages persisted in charging the opening so bravely defended by Thornt Hamby. He would bring down one or two bucks at every charge. The elder Hamby was now wounded and had fallen across a bed. While lying as he had fallen, he discovered the fiery eyes of one of the red warriors. He called for a sixshooter and, although badly wounded, his aim was steady. The Indian fell. He was perhaps the commander, as a retreat was at once ordered.

Thus ended this little sanguinary contest. In the opening of the battle, the women and children were made to lie on the floor and, in this way, all were saved. Dr. Wilson, George Bragg and the negro boy were killed, and the elder Hamby wounded. Quite a number of Indians were slain. Thornt Hamby said that in one of the forts they abandoned, there was quite a large amount of sugar on hand, which was thought to have fallen into the hands of the Indians. It was proposed to put a bottle or two of strychnine into the sugar, but for humane or economic reasons, it was not done. Had they poisoned the sugar, the Elm Creek raid would have ended, as the Indians actually captured and ate much of it.

From Bragg's Fort the Comanches proceeded to Murray's Fort, but fifteen rangers ran in on them and drew them away from that place. Five of the rangers were killed. The Indians from here turned northwest. They carried with them thousands of head of stock which they evidently intended to sell to the Federal Army. As proof, on one occasion when two or three Indians were pursuing a man named Wooten, knowing that his gun was unloaded and that he had no means of defense, they were pressing him just to see him run. He was on foot, as his horse had been killed. They taunted him by saying, "Run, Wooten, run! We know when you drive beef to Cooper! Now Comanche drive beef to Cooper!" Large numbers of both cattle and horses were secured in this way, and many of them were run north and sold. The ruthless speculator grew rich at the expense of innocent blood.

The United States government, whether intentionally or not, permitted this cruelty. It might have been the policy of that hated demon, War, but such cruelty is not recognized in war among civilized nations. The savages were remunerated, the speculator filled his coffers and the government encouraged it by purchasing the stolen stock. It is just for our government to state that she has recently paid out large sums of money to old settlers to compensate them for losses sustained during this destructive and perilous period. Many a pioneer of the Lone Star State had grown independent by privation and labor, but suddenly he finds all swept away from him, even his wife and children scalped or captives of a people who know no sympathy, but delight in the flow of blood and cries of suffering. Since these particular atrocities were brought about by that fearful war, the writer cannot refrain from explaining in his feeble way some of his feelings concerning that cruel monster. It is corruption; it is the cultivation of the most vicious inclinations of our nature; it is descending to the level of the most brutal beasts that hide in the jungles of India; it crushes all pity and love, and plants instead malice, selfishness and hatred. We censure, blame and abuse the other party. Perhaps all we needed to encourage like deeds was the chance. General Sherman's definition is correct...none can ever be better: "War is hell."

Negro Brit's Family

This family deserves special mention. They were far above the average of their race. Brit and his wife were both practical and of superior common sense. They were trusted by their owners. Mr. Johnson allowed Brit to have property of his own and, as a result, he had accumulated quite a stock of horses and cattle. Many privileges were allowed him.

Long after the capture of his family, he would make frequent trips in his effort to find them. My father-in-law, who was a resident of Wise County, owned a number of negroes. Brit, on his exploring trips, frequently stopped in to visit with them. As such, many facts were obtained from him, particularly concerning the rescue of his family, who were captured in the Elm Creek raid. For some time after this, Brit remained a slave. When he freedom was given him, by the assistance of his former master, he became even more active in his search.

Brit had obtained some hints as to his family's location and was eagerly making his way in that direction when he came upon some captured white children. True to his nature, he immediately commenced negotiations for the return of these two white children whose home was in Wise County. Their father, with the assistance of his neighbors, soon got together the forty head of horses required and with Brit's assistance, the exchange was effected. One of these boys was so taken with the Indian life that he manifested a great desire to return to them and it was with great difficulty that he was restrained. So far as is known, he was never entirely satisfied with civilized life. Brit's assistance in restoring these boys to their parents proved a great benefit to him, as many on that account were ready to render him aid in recovering his own family.

Brit soon arranged for a more perilous and longer journey than he'd ever undertaken before. This was just after the end of the Civil War in 1865. He secured the best horse to be found—a splendid black gelding, quiet and docile, yet noted for his speed. Brit took a second horse upon which he packed his bedding and provisions, as well as trinkets to trade with the Indians. Thus equipped, he started for the Panhandle, not less than two hundred miles distant.

His route was through a wild, unsettled region. He made the entire journey without seeing a single individual—friend or foe. He finally came to a place where he found the Indians had been hunting and killing game very recently. He found a very secluded spot where he could safely lariat his horses on the luxurious grass. His horses secured, he sought a place where he could overlook the surrounding country without being observed. Just as he had secured his new position, Brit spied a lone Indian riding leisurely along not far away. He came out from his concealed position into the open country and beckoned the Indian to come to him. He had learned to speak the Comanche language while that tribe was on the reservation near his ranch and was able to make his wishes known to the Indian.

Brit told the Comanche that he wanted to see his wife and children, that he liked to hunt and kill game, and that he wanted to come and live with them. The Indian promised that he would go to his people and would return to tell him what the decision was. Although it was but a few miles, the Indian did not return until the next day, when he took Brit to their camp. Brit was not permitted, however, to see his family for several days. He remained, taking on the constant risk of being killed, but all the while gaining their confidence. His devotion to his family was greater than his fear of death. He soon gained the Comanches' confidence completely, and he and his family were sent with a party on a hunting expedition.

With regarding to the hunting expedition, I will follow Captain Barry's account. He says that Brit, being an expert hunter, a good horseman and having all those qualities that make a good frontiersmen, soon became very valuable to the Indians and was allowed unusual liberty among them. Finally, this hunting party dropped down to within one hundred miles of the settlements and to a region of country that Brit was well acquainted with. He seized this opportunity and soon managed to get his family together, making a break for the settlements which he reached in safety.

There is a different account given by others, which agrees with the statements made by the negroes of my father-in-law. It is that Brit was not permitted to see his family on his first visit, as related in the preceding account, but that he approached them as described above. They held a council and agreed with him to release his family for a certain number of ponies. He then returned home and his friends among the white people assisted him in getting up the number required. He delivered the ponies to Fort Sill where the exchange was made and returned home with his family where he had care of the ranch until 1871.

Brit always seemed to enjoy telling his exploits among the Indians and especially relating his thrilling experiences in securing the release of his family. It was interesting to listen to him. He had made a study of the habits, customs and characteristics of the red man. Had he been willing to remain with them, he could have been a leader among them, but his only thought was to return and again be in charge of that ranch. But, alas, he was not permitted to enjoy that privilege very long. In the early spring of 1871, he went to Weatherford for supplies. He had with him two other negroes who worked with him on the range. They were all well armed and were each driving a team.

They went into camp near Salt Creek. They were not aware, but there was another train not far from them. When the members of this train were rounding their teams the next morning, they saw about twenty-five Indians gallop upon a ridge about half a mile distant from them. About this time, they heard the roar of guns back by the road, which proved to be at Brit's camp. The Indians seen on the ridge at once rushed in the direction of the firing.

Brit and his companions sold their lives as dearly as possible. The teamsters of the other train witnessed this fight from start to finish. They stated that Brit's two companions fell in the first and second charges made on his camp.

Brit kept up the fight for a long time. The enemy made many charges. Some of their number, from the bullets of Brit's rifle, fell at each charge. As a last resort, Brit was seen to kill his favorite horse and use him for a breastwork. It was supposed at that time that he was wounded. He fired several times from his new position. When his gun was at last silenced, the Indians rushed into his camp, cut off his right arm, cut out his heart, clipped his ears and scalped him. They then pillaged the camp, gathered together their dead and wounded, and left without making an attack on the other camp. They had enough to do to tend to their dead and wounded. When the teamsters from the other train ventured into Brit's camp, they found one hundred cartridge shells—proof that he had made a desperate fight.

Where Captain Fields' wagon train was captured and burned, a monument has been built to commemorate the bravery and gallantry of those who fell in that contest. Why not place one on the spot where brave Brit fell? Though dark in color, his heart was white. He probably slew more savages than the whole of Captain Fields' train. No one familiar with the circumstances doubts that the Indians knew whom they were fighting. They were doubtless on this special raid to kill Brit. He was well known to them as a successful and desperate Indian fighter. May the memory of his noble deeds find a lodgment in the hearts of men and may his soul be in that land where wars and the tribulations of this life cannot enter.

Big Foot Wallace

As early as 1850, when my father moved to Dallas County, the name of Big Foot Wallace was often spoken. He was then regarded as a great Indian fighter. He was in a number of hard-fought battles while the Texas Republic was struggling against the Mexicans for her independence. The writer well remembers sitting by a log fire and listening to the stories, told by Captain William Coombes and other old setters, of Big Foot Wallace, Ellis P. Bean, David Crockett and Ben Milam. At this time, Wallace was the most noted. He was one of the Mier prisoners, but fortunately drew a white bean. He rendered valuable service during the Mexican War, and was in the frontier in the capture of the old Capital of the Montezumas.

After the close of this war, he was made captain of the Texas Rangers. The United States mail line from San Antonio to El Paso was placed in his charge. This was, perhaps, the most dangerous service in which he had ever engaged. People were being murdered continuously on this route by both Mexicans and Indians. It would be impossible to give anything resembling a correct account of all his adventures and narrow escapes. Partly from memory and partly from other written accounts, only a few of the more important events will be given here.

John Henry Brown, in his fine work, does not mention Big Foot Wallace. He gives others credit for their fine service but fails to mention this great hero, noted in both Indian and Mexican warfare. Wallace was not only the hero of many battles, but performed in like manner in several hand-to-hand fights. He was once out with a surveying party in what is now Palo Pinto County. By some means, he became separated from his companions. The Indians discovered him, but he managed to elude them by hiding in a cave among the rocks. He spent the night in comparative safety. The next morning, he started on his journey homeward, but sprained his ankle and was compelled to return to his cave. He was unable to travel and, forced to remain for three or four weeks, he lived on pecans and whatever game he could kill.

When he was sufficiently recovered, he set out again for the settlements. On his way, he was captured by the Indians. They held a council of war and decided to burn him at the stake. After Wallace was bound and the wood was piled up around him, an old squaw and a young chief, Black Wolf, came to his relief. By their pleadings, his life was saved. He remained with them some time before an opportunity presented itself for escape. He reached his home in safety.

Some time after this, he located a ranch on the Medina River, just above San Antonio. He soon found himself in comfortable circumstances, surrounded by his cattle and horses. When the country began to settle, he availed himself of his rights as an old settler. When he had gathered the comforts of life around him, a land shark pried out an error in his title. His land was thus unjustly taken from him and, for a long while, he was a wanderer over South Texas. After the lapse of some time, appreciative and sympathizing friends enlisted themselves in his behalf, and his land was restored to him by a special act of the Legislature. His injury was much talked of at the time and the sentiment around most likely influenced the Legislature.

Wilbarger, in his *Indian Depredations in Texas*, gives many interesting stories from a little book, *The Adventures of Big Foot Wallace*. They are given in Wallace's own language. From his own lingo, we can better understand the man. Wallace said: "I have been in many tight places, but when I was in charge of the mail line extending from San Antonio to El Paso, I got into one that I thought I would never squeeze out of it, but I did, as I have gotten out of all the scrapes that I have been in since coming to Texas.

"I never was severely wounded, either by an arrow or a ball, which, considering my size, I regard as very wonderful. I have known many men like Generals Scott and Johnson who had an unfortunate knack of getting wounded in every fight they went into, but I have not been of that sort. They say that one born to be hung will not get shot or drowned. That accounts for my good luck; but I am flying off of my story before I have fairly commenced it.

"We had been traveling since about twelve o'clock at night, in order to reach the watering place on Devil's River, where I intended to noon and graze our animals for two or three hours. At daylight, I noticed several Indian smokes rising up and disappearing, but they were apparently a long way off. We had crossed an Indian trail where fifteen or twenty horses had passed. I did not like the sign, so told the boys to keep a sharp lookout, as I was satisfied that the Indians were hatching up some kind of devilment for our benefit.

"We, however, reached the water hole in safety. About noon, we watered our horses and hoppled them out for grass. I had eighteen men with me, who were mostly frontiersmen who had seen good service, and who were good Indian fighters, for I had seen them tried. They were as good as ever drew bead on an Indian. There was only one tenderfoot. There was about a quarter of an acre in chaparral brush near the water hole and, after we had taken a bite to eat, I told the boys to draw the coach up to the edge of the thicket and then they could lie down on their blankets and take a snooze, for they had been awake all the night before, and were pretty well worn out.

"I felt badly fagged myself, but somehow uneasiness pervaded me so I could not sleep, though I had seen nothing in particular to excite my suspicion since we had stopped at the watering place. I felt uneasy, and determined to watch while the others slept. If there had been nothing else, the appearance of the country around our encampment was enough to make one uneasy, for it had a real suffering look. It was made up of rocks and hills, with here and there little clumps of thorny bushes, stunted cedars, with narrow little valleys and canyons between them. There was no kind of vegetation but paths of withered grass upon which our horses were picking a scant repast.

"We could see but a short distance in any direction. I picked up my rifle and walked off about fifty yards to a little mound to the right of our camp, where I could have the best view if the enemy approached. I don't know how it is with others, but there are times when I feel low-spirited and depressed without being able to account for the feeling. Such was my condition at this time. The breeze rustled with a melancholy sound through the dead grass and stunted bushes. The howling of a solitary coyote sounded to me unusually mournful.

"The only sound beside this which would be heard was the snoring of Ben Wade in the camp, some distance away. He was the most provident of men, especially when any eating or sleeping was to be done. Ben's motto was, 'Never refuse to eat or sleep when you are on the plains, if you have a chance. This is the only way to keep up and stand the racket a long time.' Before I proceed, I must depart a little and pay my compliments to Ben. He could eat more and sleep more than any man I ever messed with in camp. When he was on the plains, he would eat forty times a day if the chance presented itself. 'It may be,' said Ben, 'that it will be forty days before we get any more.' He continued, 'By this method, I can do without a long time.' Ben was always on hand when there was anything to eat, and the moment he was off guard, you could hear him snoring like a wild mule.

"One night Ben and I went on a spying expedition in one of the villages of the Wacos. Their dogs discovered us, and their barking soon aroused the whole Indian tribe. In a little while, they began to pour out of their lodges, ready for a fight with their bows and arrows. We concluded about that time that we could find a healthier climate. We made for the river, about two miles away. As we passed the Indian lodge, Ben discovered some buffalo ribs roasting in front of the fire. 'Cap,' says Ben, 'let's stop and eat a bite; there's no telling when we will get another chance.' At that very moment, we could hear the red devils yelling behind us like a pack of hungry wolves.

"'Well,' said I, 'if you want to sell your life for a mess of pottage, you can stop, but I set a higher value on mine, and can't tarry just now.'

"'But Cap,' said he, 'it is a rule I always stick to—never to let a chance slip of taking a bite when I am on the warpath, and I do not want to break through it at this late day.' Seeing that I made no sign of stopping, some of the Indians being then within a hundred yards of us, screaming like so many catamounts, he said, 'If you won't wait, I must take the ribs along with me.' I wish I may be cut into bait for mudcats if he didn't sling them over his shoulder, though a half dozen of the foremost red skins were in sight of us!

"Ben and I were pretty hard to beat in a foot race those days, but on this occasion they caused us to put in our best licks for about a mile and a half. The darkness of the night was in our favor. We finally reached the river bottom in safety and, being out of immediate danger, I said to Ben, 'As you would take the ribs, I will take one of them, as my run has given me an appetite.'

"'Sorry, Cap,' he said, 'but you spoke too late. I've polished them all.' Ben had picked the ribs as clean as my ivory-handled sixshooter. While he ate and slept more than his part, he was as true as ever fluttered and would do to tie to in time of danger.

"Ben was lying asleep while I was out on the little mound watching around but, thinking he had slept enough, I determined to wake him and get him to help me bring in the horses and mules. Just at that moment, I saw one of the horses raise his head and look in one direction for some time. Soon after, I saw a deer running as if something had frightened him. I waited to see that there were no wolves after him, then hurried to camp and gave Ben a shake by the shoulder. In a low voice, I told him to get up, for I did not wish to wake the other boys.

"'Hello,' he said raising himself on one hand and rubbing his eyes with the other. 'Hello, Cap, what's the matter? Is dinner ready?'

"'No,' said I. 'You cormorant! It hasn't been a half hour

since you ate dinner enough for six men. Get up and help me bring in the horses.'

"'Indians about?' asked Ben. 'If I did not know you so well I would say that you were over cautious. But if you say bring in the horses, here goes.'

"We brought them all and lariated them all securely in the chaparral thicket without waking any of the other boys. There being no other signs of Indians, Ben lay down again to finish his nap. Scarcely had he coiled himself in his blankets when he sprang up as quickly as if a stinging lizard had wounded him. 'Cracky!' said he. 'Cap, I hear their horses' feet! They are comin'!' I listened attentively and, sure enough, I could hear the clatter of their horses' feet on the rocky ground. The next minute, I saw twenty Comanche warriors coming toward our camp as fast as their horses could bring them.

"We aroused the boys in an instant and were ready for them. The Comanches had evidently expected to take us by surprise. They never checked their horses until they were within a few feet of the chaparral in which we were posted. They began at once to pour in their dogwood switches among us as thick as hail. We returned the compliment so effectually with our rifles and sixshooters that they soon fell back, taking with them four of their dead warriors. One one of our men was slightly wounded—a Mr. Fry. One of our mules was killed.

"They disappeared behind a hill and most of our men thought they had gone for good. I told them that they were mistaken and that we would have a lively time of it yet, and that they had only gone off to dismount. They would soon be back and give us another turn. We had not more than reloaded our sixshooters and rifles when they rose up all around the little thicket, yelling and screeching as if we were all a set of greenhorns to be frightened by such a racket. However, I saw very plainly that they were in earnest this time.

"I told Ben Wade to take three of the boys and keep them from the far side of the thicket, while I kept them at bay on the side next to the coach. We had our hands full, I can tell you. I think we killed one of their noted chiefs in the first charge they made on us. They seemed now bent on revenge. I never saw the red rascals come so boldly up to the scratch before. Three or four more times they charged us with great spirit. Once they got right among us and it became a hand-to-hand fight. The boys never flinched but their sixshooter bullets among the Indians flew so fast that they could stand it but a little while. They soon retreated behind the hill.

"When the Indians were charging us the second time, I saw one of my men skulk behind a bunch of prickly pears. I went to him and told him to come out and fight like a man. He replied, 'I would, Cap, if I could. But I can't stand it.'

"I saw by the way his lips quivered and his hands shook that he was speaking the truth. 'Well, stay here and then I will say nothing about it,' I said but some of the others had seen him and had I not interfered, they would have killed him. He might as well have been killed, for the poor fellow had no peace after this.

"I have seen two or three men in my life that were natural cowards. They could no more help it than they could help having bandy legs or a snub nose. They are born so, and are not to be blamed but pitied. You might as well blame a man for not being as smart as Henry Clay, or for not being as brave as Julius Caesar. All the same, it is very aggravating to have them act in that way when the service of every man is so badly needed, as on this occasion. Bravery is about as safe from harm as cowardice. This man was the only one wounded, except Fry. An arrow flew where he was hiding and pinned him to the ground.

"When the Indians retreated a second time, the boys thought again that the fight was over, but I told them that I did not think so; that they would try to delude us into the belief that they were gone, when in fact they would be waiting for us to start our journey. I told them that we could soon satisfy ourselves as to their intentions. I ordered every man to take his gun and lie down under the coach, and keep perfectly quiet. The boys soon began to grow tired of their positions—all but Ben who was fast asleep.

"We saw an Indian cautiously poke his head out of the chaparral about seventy yards from where we were. He looked for a long time toward us and, seeing no signs of life, he ventured out and straightened up to have a better view. 'Don't fire, boys,' said I. 'There will be more of them out directly and we can get two or three of them.'

"In a little while, another Indian came out and stood by the first. And then another, and so on, until there were five of them in a row standing side by side, all looking intently toward the coach and wondering, I suppose, what had become of us. 'Now score them, boys!' said I, and we let them have it. Four of them fell dead, and the fifth scrambled back into the brush as fast as he could. I ordered the men to reload, telling them that more would appear presently to carry off their dead but I was mistaken that time.

"Nothing was seen of them for ten or fifteen minutes, when we saw an arm rise out of the chaparral and make a motion. In a minute, one of the dead Indians was snaked into the thicket. I wish I may be kicked to death by a grasshopper, if they didn't rope every one of them and drag them off in that way. We never saw a thing but that Indian's arm motioning back and forth as he threw his lasso. 'Boggy,' says I, 'that gits me. I've been in a good many scrimmages with the Indians but I never saw them snake off their dead in that way before. However, it shows that they have had enough of the fight. I think now that we might venture to make a start without fear of being interrupted by them again.'

"While the boys were hitching up their horses, I took my rifle and went out for the purpose of reconnoitering, and well for us that I did, for on reaching the top of the little rise, where I had first taken my stand, I counted forty warriors coming down a canyon not more than four hundred yards away. I was satisfied that it was not the same party that we had been fighting, but a reinforcement coming to their assistance.

"When they arrived within one hundred yards of where I was sitting, I rose and showed myself to them. Instantly they halted. One of them, who I suppose was the chief, rode thirty or forty yards in advance of the rest and asked me in Mexican, which most Comanches speak, what we were doing there. There is nothing like keeping a stiff upper lip and showing a bold front when dealing with Indians, so I told him that we had been fighting with the Comanches and had flogged them genteelly, too. 'Yes,' he said, 'you are a sneaking lot of coyotes and are afraid to come out of the brush and fight us. You are afraid to travel the road. You are all squaws. You dare not poke your noses out of the chaparral.'

"'If you will wait till we eat dinner,' I answered, 'we will show you whether we are afraid to travel the road or not. We shall camp tonight at California Springs in spite of the whole Comanche Nation!' With this remark, I turned and walked slowly back to the coach as if I thought they were not worth bothering with any further. I was satisfied that if I could make them believe that we did not fear them, and that we intended to camp at California Springs that night, that they would hurry on there for the purpose of waylaying us at or near that place. I was right, for they immediately set out for the springs, eight miles distant, leaving three Indians to watch our movements.

"When I got back to the coach, I told the boys what I had said to the supposed chief, and there was no doubt they would hasten on to that place. I informed them of my plan. We would wait until the Comanches had time enough to reach the springs, then we would take the back track to Fort Clark. 'They are too strong for us, boys,' said I, 'for they have had a reinforcement of forty warriors. They will fight like fury to revenge the death of those we have killed.'

"'Cap,' said Ben Wade, 'I heard you make one sensible remark to that red skin you were talking with.'

"'What was that, Ben?' I asked.

"'You told him as soon as we got dinner, we would go to California Springs in spite of the Comanche Nation.'

"'Yes,' I said, 'I told him that because I wanted him to think we were delaying here on our own accord and not because we were afraid of them. I believe they have gone off with that impression.'

"'It was a pretty smart dodge in you, Cap, to put them off on the wrong track in that way, I'll admit. We may not get to California Springs after all, but we can eat dinner. We had better do what's in our power. Besides, Cap,' he continued, hunting out a piece of venison and some hard tack, 'they have likely left a spy to watch us. You told him we would eat before we left, so I will make a pretense to take a bite so that the chief will not have reason to think we are throwing off on him.'

"'There will be no danger of that, Ben, if he is where he can see you. There is no throw-off in you when there is eating or sleeping to be done,' I said.

"'Nor fighting, either,' he added. 'If I hadn't shot that Indian on the last charge they made on us, just as he was drawing his bow on you, not six feet away, you would have had a quill sticking in you as long as a porcupine's.'

"'That's a fact, Ben, and it's not the first time you have done me a good turn. I am not the man to forget. When we get to Fort Clark, we will lay over a day, just to give you a chance to lay in a good stock of provender.' Ben was satisfied and, as soon as he had finished his venison, he turned over and was fast asleep. After waiting about half an hour longer, we took the back track to Fort Clark. We made all the speed possible. Just as we started, we saw two Indians put off toward the springs. No doubt they had been left to watch our movements. The other, for there were three, followed us at a safe distance from our rifles, for seven or eight miles, when he disappeared. We had so much of a start on them, and the road was so good, they had no chance to overtake us if they followed—and they did. We reached Fort Clark the next morning, where our wounded were cared for. The commander at the fort furnished us an escort of twelve men and a sergeant. We then made the trip to San Antonio without further trouble.

"In the fall of 1842, the Indians were worse on the frontier than they had been before or since. You couldn't take a horse out at night with any expectation of finding him the next morning. A fellow's scalp was not safe when he was outside his own shack. The people living at the front at last came to the conclusion that something had to be done, or they would be compelled to fall back to the settlements, which would have been reversing the order of things. We came together, by agreement, at my ranch and organized a company of forty men.

"The next time the Indians came down from the mountains, we took the trail, determined to follow it as long as our horses could hold out. The trail led us toward the headwaters of the Llano River. On the third day out, I discovered a lot of signal smokes rising up a long distance off in the direction we were going. That night, we camped near a water hole and put out a double guard. Just before the sun went down, I discovered a smoke not more than three miles away to the northeast of us. I felt sure that there was a party of Indians encamped there. I went to the captain and asked permission to leave camp about three or four hours before daybreak. My purpose was to find out if there were Indians there. The captain instructed the guard to let me pass at any hour I wished.

"I whetted up old butcher a little and rammed two bullets down old Sweet Lips, and left camp about two hours before daylight, going in the direction I had seen the smoke the day before. The chaparral was as thick in some places as the hair on a dog's back, but I worked my way through it about a mile and a half. I then came to a deep canyon that headed in the way I had seen the smoke. I scrambled down into it and waited for day to break, then slowly and cautiously continued my course along the bottom of the canyon. It was crooked and in some places so narrow that two men could scarcely travel side by side.

"At length, I came to a place where the canyon made a sudden turn. Just as I turned the corner, I came plump up against a big Indian, who was coming down the canyon,

I supposed, to spy on our camp. We were both stooping down when we met. Our heads came together with considerable force. The Indian rolled one way and I the other. We rose about the same time. So unexpected was the encounter that both of us stood for a moment, uncertain what to do, and glared at each other like two catamounts when disputing the carcass of a deer. The Indian had a gun, as did I, but we were in too close quarters to use them. It seemed as if both of us came to the same conclusion at the same time.

"We dropped our rifles and grappled, saying not a word. You see, boys, I am a pretty stout man, yet. But in those days, without meaning to brag, I do not believe there was a man west of the Colorado River who could stand against me in a regular catamount, bear-hug, hand-to-hand fight. The minute I had hefted that Indian, I knew I had a job that would bring the sweat, and perhaps the blood. He was nearly as tall as I. I am six feet two or three inches. He weighed about one hundred and seventy-five pounds, net, for he had no clothes on worth mentioning. I had some advantage in weight. He was wiry, as active as a cat and as slick as an eel, which is no wonder for he was greased from head to foot with bear's oil.

"At it we went, without a word being spoken, and in dead earnest; up one side of the canyon, then down to the bottom. The dust flew in such volumes that had one been passing along the bank, they would have supposed that a whirlwind was raging below. I could throw him easily but the moment he struck the ground, the varmint would give himself a twist like a snake and pop right up and on top of me. I could not hold him still for a minute because he was so slick with bear grease. Each one of us was busy trying to draw his butcher knife from its sheath all the time, but it seemed that neither could succeed.

"At last I found my breath failing. I came to the conclusion that if I did not do something soon, I should have my note taken. The Indian was like a Lobo wolf, and was getting better all the time. I gave him a backhanded trip that brought his head against a sharp rock that was sticking up out of the ground. He was completely stunned by this shock. Before he fairly came to, I snatched my knife from its sheath and drove it with all my strength up to its hilt in his body. When he felt the cold steel, he threw me from him as if I had been a ten year old child. He sprang upon me before I could rise, drew his own knife, and raised it above my head with the intention of plunging it into my body.

"I tell you what, boys, I often see that Indian now in my dreams—particularly after eating a hearty supper of bear meat and honey—grappling me with his left hand, his butcher knife raised in the right, his two piercing eyes gleaming like a panther's in the dark. It is astonishing how fast a man can think under such circumstances. He thinks faster than words can fly along one of these newfangled telegraph wires. I looked toward the blue sky above me and bid it a long farewell, and at the green trees and sparkling waters and bright sun. I thought of my mother as I remembered her when I was a small boy. I thought of the old home, the apple orchard and the little brook where I used to fish for minnows. I considered the commons over which I had galloped on my pony, and of the blue eyed, partridge-built young woman I had a leaning to, who had lived down in the Yumwatt settlement. All these and many more thoughts flashed across my mind while that knife was gleaming above my breast.

"All at once, the Indian gave a keen yell, and down went the knife with such force that it went to the hilt in the hard ground beside me. The last time I had thrown him down, a deep gash had been cut across his forehead by a sharp-pointed rock, and the blood was streaming down over his eyes. It so blinded him that he missed his mark. I fully expected that he would repeat the blow, but he lay still and made no effort to draw his knife from the ground. I looked at his eyes and saw that they were closed tight and fast. There was a kind of devilish grin about his mouth as if he, though dead, was still thinking that he had sent me to the 'happy hunting ground.'

"I threw him from me. He tumbled to the bottom of the canyon, dead. My knife had gone to his heart. I looked at him for some time, lying there so still and stiffening so fast in the cool morning air. I spoke to myself as follows: 'Well, old fellow, you made a good fight of it, and if luck had not been against you, you would have certainly taken my sign and Alice Ann would have lost the best string she had in her bow. And now, old fellow, I will do for you what I never did for an Indian before. I am going to give you a good Christian burial.'

"I broke his gun into a dozen pieces and laid them beside him, according to Indian custom, so it might be of use to him in the 'happy hunting ground,' but if they have no first class smiths in that land, I don't think it will be of much use any time soon. Then I pulled up some pieces of rock from the canyon and piled them around him until he was safe from the attacks of coyotes and other animals. His bones, no doubt, are there till this day. This is a true account of my fight with the big Indian in the canyon."

When I came to Texas fifty years ago, these stories were being told about Big Foot Wallace and believed to be facts.

Wallace's Maverick

This, as the preceding account, is given in Wallace's own language, in 1867:

"Indian are sometimes monstrously independent. They will run the greatest risks without anything to gain by it. You would hardly believe that about six months ago, a party of Tonkawa warriors came within half a mile of my ranch, and in broad daylight killed one of my fattest mavericks (unmarked yearlings), pitched their camp and set in for a general jollification.

"It happened that morning that Tom Jones, Bill Dukes and Jeff Bonds, with myself, were out after stock, when all at once Jeff remarked that he smelled meat roasting on the coals. I turned my nose windward and smelled it too, as plainly as I have ever smelled fried middling on a frosty morning, with the breeze about dead ahead, when I've been coming in after a three or four hours' hunt before breakfast. Talk about your Hostetter's Bitters and patent tonics. The best tonic I have ever known was a three hour hunt among the hills on a frosty morning. It gives a fellow an appetite that nothing less than a mule and a hamper of greens can satisfy.

"Well, as I was saying, just as soon as I smelled the roasted beef, I knew that there were Indians about. It was the last place I would have looked, had I been hunting them. Still, I was sure they were there, for catamounts, coyotes and panthers always take their meats raw. I told the boys to keep quiet and to get down and fasten their horses. We recapped our guns and sixshooters, then carefully crept along in the bushes until we discovered the Indians not more than fifty yards from us. There, they were making themselves as much at home and as comfortable around their fire as if they were in the mountains on the head of the Guadalupe River, which undoubtedly is the roughest scope of country in Texas.

"I whispered to Jeff Bonds, who was nearest me, and said, 'Well, don't this beat you?! Did you ever see such impudence before in your life? To kill one of my fattest mavericks and barbecue it in half a mile of my ranch in broad daylight! Well, if I don't let him know that I am landlord of these diggins yet, and bring in a bill for the entertainment they have had, you may call me short stock, even if I do stand six foot three in my stockings!'

"All this time, the Indians never suspected that we were near them. There was one big fellow among them that must have been six feet two or three inches high in his stockings, though, of course, he never had on a pair in his life. He was making very prominent around the fire, broiling steaks out of my maverick, turning and toasting the joints of the spits, all the while talking and laughing, just as though he did not know that he was within half a mile of Big Foot Wallace's ranch.

"I don't think I ever felt less like giving quarters, but once, in my life. That was when a big nigger with a nose like dormer window, and a pair of lips that looked like he had been sucking a bee gum and had gotten badly stung in the operation, objected to my registering as a voter. He was one of the board of registrars at Clarksville. He was not in a condition to object to anyone else registering that day or the next. I took him a club over the head which would have stunned a beef steer, but he never even winked. I changed my tactics and gave him twelve inches of shoe leather on the shin. That brought him to his milk in short order. The bureau fined me fifty dollars and costs, but the amount has not been settled yet and probably never will be, until they can get a crowd that is good at traveling and fighting Indians to pilot the sheriff to my ranch.

"I will return to the Indians that were barbecuing my maverick. I intended to take the fellow, making himself so prominent around the fire, in my special keeping. I whispered to Jeff to draw a bead on the one sitting down, and told Bill and Sam to shoot the other three standing up. At a word, all four of our rifles cracked at the same time. Just as I drew the trigger, the big Indian was lifting a chunk of my maverick from the fire. At the crack of the rifle, the chunk of meat flew up in the air, the big Indian pitched forward, face first, into the coals and ashes. Before we left, there was again the strong smell of roasted meat, but it was no my maverick this time.

"Jeff killed his Indian dead in his tracks, but only one of the other two was wounded and then only slightly. They retreated to the chaparral and we never saw them again. We got all their bows and arrows, and one new flintlock steel rifle. To give the scamps their dues, they clearly understood roasting beef to perfection. The maverick was fine. We gave it a thorough test. The big Indian must have been a kind of chief, for he had about twenty pounds of brass rings on his arms, and a cue that reached down to his heels. The other Indians took the hint and never camped on my premises again."

Big Foot Wallace & The Indian Hater

"Did I tell you of a curious character that I fell in with in the Yumwatt settlement on the Lavaca River, a year or two after I came to Texas?" asks Big Foot Wallace. "I have met with many a good Indian hater in my time, but this fellow hated Indians with such a vim that he hadn't room left for a good appetite. He had a good reason for his hatred. If they had served me as they did him, I'm afraid I would have taken to scalping for a livelihood, instead of just ripping one now and then.

"A party of us had been out on an exploring expedition on the Nueces River, which was then almost unknown to Americans. The night we got back to the Lavaca, we camped on its western bank and went to sleep without the usual precaution of putting out a guard, thinking we were near enough the settlements to be safe from an attack from the Indians. I told the boys that I thought we were running a great risk in not having a guard out. I had learned from experiences that, where you least expect them, they are most apt to be. But the boys were all tired from their long day's ride, and thought there was no danger. If there was, they were willing to take the chances.

"After we had got some supper and staked our horses, we wrapped our blankets about us and soon were fast asleep. I was the first one to rouse up about daylight. Looking in the direction we had staked our horses, I discovered that they were all gone. I rose quietly without waking any of the boys and went out to reconnoiter the 'sign.' I had gone but a little ways on the prairie when I picked up an arrow. A little further on, I came on one of our horses dead on the grass, with a dozen dogwood switches sticking into different parts of his body. This satisfied me at once that the Indians had paid us a social visit during the night and with the exception of the one that they had killed (an unruly beast), they had carried off all our stock.

"I went back to camps, stirred up the boys and gave them the pleasing information that we were ten miles from food and water, and were flat afoot. It was no use to cry, so we held a council of war, as to what was to be done under the circumstances. It was decided that each man was to shoulder his own plunder, or leave it, as he liked, and that we should take a bee line for the settlement above us on the river. There, we would borrow horses if we could and follow the Indians and take back from them the horses they had stolen from us.

"We hastily ate a snack. Each man shouldered his burden and we set out for the settlement. It was a pretty fatiguing trip, hampered as we were with our guns and rigging, but we made it in good time. Fortunately, a man had just come in with a large cavayard of horses. When we made our situation known to him, he told us to go into the yard and select the horses we wanted. They were only about half broke. It took us about an hour to saddle them, and about fifteen minutes to get on their backs. I was luckier than the other boys, only getting two kicks and one bite before I mounted mine.

"When all were ready, we put spurs to our horses and galloped back to our camp of the previous night. We took the trail of the Indians, which was plainly visible in the rank grass that grew at the time along the river bottoms. Several of the men who lived in the settlement came with us. We were all captains, colonels and majors, except for one chap who was a judge. Our company numbered thirteen, all armed and mounted. As long as the Indians kept to the valley, we had no trouble in following their trail, and made good time in their pursuit.

"When we had trailed them eight or ten miles, I had to halt and dismount, for the purpose of fixing my girth, which by some means had come unfastened. While thus engaged, I heard the tramp of horse hooves behind me on the way we had come. I saw a man riding rapidly on our trail. When he got where I was, he reined his horse, evidently intending to wait for me. I had a chance of observing as curious a specimen of human kind as I had ever seen in any country. He was a tall, well-built chap, dressed in a buckskin suit, hunting shirt, leggins and had on a coonskin cap. He had an old-fashioned flint and steel Kentucky rifle on his shoulder. He had a tomahawk and scalping knife in his belt. His hair was matted and hung around his shoulder in long rolls. His eyes peered out from among them as bright as two mesquite coals.

"I have seen all sorts of eyes—panthers', wolves', cata-mounts', leopards' and Mexican lions'—but I never saw eyes that glittered and danced like this man's. He was mounted on an ugly, rough, raw-boned, lazy-looking horse with a heavy mane and tail. Though, with half an eye, anyone could tell he would do to depend on in a pinch. As soon as I had patched up my girth, I mounted and rode along rather sociable with this curious specimen for a mile or two with-out ever a word passing between us. I soon tired of this, and although I felt a little suspicious of this strange-looking animal, I mustered up the courage and made a pass at him.

"'Are you a stranger in these parts?' said I.

"'Not exactly,' he replied. 'I have been here off and on for about three years. I know every water hole from here to the Rio Grande, especially those used by the Indians in their coming and going.'

"'Aren't you afraid to travel alone so much in this coun-try?' I asked.

"He grinned a sort of sickly smile; his fingers clutched the handle of his tomahawk; his eyes danced a perfect jig. He said, 'No. The Indians are more afraid of me than I of them. If they knew that I was waylaying a certain trail, they would go forty miles out of the way to give me a wide berth. The trouble is they never know where to find me. The best horse in the country can't come along beside old Pepper-Pod, when I want him to work in the lead.' As he said this, he gave old Pepper-Pod a smart touch with his spurs, and the horse made a vicious plunge and started off like a shot out of a gun. Pepper-Pod was soon reined in. We rode in silence for some time.

"Again I spoke. 'Man of a family, I suppose?' Gracious! If a ten-pounder had been fired off at my ear, I couldn't have been more astonished than I was at the chap's actions. He turned pale, his lips quivered, he fumbled with the handle of his sixshooter, his eyes looked like two little lightning bugs on a dark night.

"He did not answer me for some time, but at last said, 'No, I have no family now. Ten years ago, I had a wife and two little boys. The Indians murdered them all in cold blood. I have got a few of them for it, and if I am spared long enough, will get a few more before I die.' As he said this, he clutched the trigger of his gun, and shaved his scalping knife up and down in the scabbard. He gave Pepper-Pod another dig in the ribs. The horse reared and plunged in a way that would have emptied that saddle of any other man than a good rider.

"After a while, he and Pepper-Pod quieted down. He spoke: 'You must not think strange of me. I can't help but get into these flurries when I think of how the Indians murdered my poor wife and little boys. I will tell you my story," said Jefferson Turner, for that was his name. 'Ten years ago, I was as happy as any man in the world. Now I am as miserable as any except when I am waylaying or scalping an Indian. It is the only satisfaction I have now. I once had a farm in Kentucky, near the mouth of the Beechfork. Though we had no money, we lived happily and comfortably with nothing to fear when we lay down at night.

"'In an unlucky hour for us, a man on his way to Texas stopped with us. He told us about the abundance of game, the many quick fortunes that had been made in this country, and the rich land. From that time I grew restless and discontented. I determined that as soon as possible I would seek my fortune in the promised land. The next fall, the opportunity presented itself for me to sell my farm for a good price. I sold it and moved to Texas.

"'After wandering about for some time, we settled on the bank of a beautiful stream that ran into the Guadalupe River. My wife left Kentucky very reluctantly, but the lovely spot that we had chosen for a home, the rich land, the beautiful scenery and the mild climate soon reconciled her to the change we had made.

"'One lovely morning in May when the sun was shining brightly and the birds were chirping in every bough, I went with my rifle for a stroll in the woods. When I left the house, my wife was at work in our little garden, singing as gayly as any of the birds. My little boys were laughing and tumbling their hoops about the yard. I had gone about a mile, entirely ignorant of any danger, when I heard a dozen guns go off at once in the direction of my home.

"'The thought flashed across my mind in a moment that the Indians were murdering my family. With speed equal to that of a frightened deer, I ran toward my home. From the direction in which I approached, the house was hidden from my view by a thick grove of elm trees that grew in front. I hastened through this and into the open door of my house. The first I saw was the dead body of my poor wife, lying pale and bloody upon the floor, with the lifeless body of my youngest boy tightly clasped in her arms. She had tried to protect him to the last. The body of my oldest boy lay close by, scalped and covered with blood from their wounds.

"'The Indians, who had left the house for some purpose, returned, not knowing that I was there. I shot one of them through the heart, and rushed at the balance like a tiger. There were a dozen of the savages, but it would have made no difference with me if there had been a thousand of them, for I cared naught for life any longer, and thought only of my loved ones.

"'I have but a faint recollection of what occurred after this. I remember hearing their yells of fright and astonishment as I rushed upon them, and I cut several of them to pieces with my butcher knife before they could escape through the door. Then all was blank, and I know nothing more. I suppose that some of them shot me from the outside of the house, which rendered me unconscious. I gave them such a scare that they never returned to the house again, or you know that they would have taken my scalp and carried off the dead Indians.

"'Some time during the day, some of the neighbors happened by the house and noticed the unusual silence that prevailed. They supposed that something was wrong, and came in, when the dreadful sight I have described met their eyes. They told me afterward that they found me lying across the dead body of an Indian, gashed and hacked with my butcher knife. My good neighbors, observing signs of life in me, took me to one of their homes, dressed my wounds and did all they could for me. For days I hovered between life and death. They thought I would never get well, but gradually my wounds healed and my strength returned. For a long time, I was not right here (tapping his head.) Even now I am more like a crazy man than a sane man. When I am compelled to go a long time without taking a scalp, I always see the bloody scalps of my wife and children.'

"'I hope, my friend,' said I, for I did not like the way his eyes danced in his head, and the careless way he had of cocking his gun and slinging it around—'I hope that you have had your regular rations today and that you do not feel disposed to take a white man's scalp, when the Indian's can't be found handy.'

"The fellow actually laughed when I said this. It was the first time I had heard anything like a laugh from him. 'Oh no,' said he, 'I have been tolerably well supplied of late and can get along tolerably comfortably for a week yet. I have forty-six of them hanging up in my camp on the Chicolite but I shan't be satisfied unless I can take a cool hundred of them before I die. I will take them, too, just as sure as my name is Jeff Turner.'

"Again his eyes glared, his hands began fumbling with his scalping knife in such a way that, if I had a drop of Indian blood in my veins, would have made me feel exceedingly shaky. To change the subject, I asked him which way he was traveling. I knew he was going along with us, of course. 'Any way these Indians go,' he replied. 'I had as soon go one direction as another. I always follow the freshest Indian trail I come across. You and your company may get tired and quit this trail, but I will follow it until I get a scalp or two to take back with me to my camp on the Chicolite.'

"By this time, we had caught up to my companions. All rode on in silence. Presently we came to a hard place in the road where the Indians had scattered. We lost the trail; not the least sign was visible. At that time, none of us had much experience in trailing and fighting Indians except Jeff Turner, the Indian hater. We soon found out that he knew more about following a trail than all of us put together. From this time on, we let him take the lead. We would follow wherever he would go.

"Sometimes, when the ground was hard and rocky, he would hesitate for awhile. The Indians would scatter and were hard to trail, but in a moment or so he was all right again, and would be off at such speed that we were compelled to keep in full gallop to keep up with him. About a half hour by sun he told us to keep sharp look out, and make no noise, as the Indian are close by. In fact, we had not traveled more than three hundred yards when we saw their blanket tents in the edge of some post oak timber, not more than a quarter of a mile away to our right. We put spurs to our horses and were soon right among them.

"They didn't see us until we were within fifty yards of their camp. They seized their guns and bows and fired at us, but did no damage but to wound one horse. We dismounted and began pouring a deadly fire into them. Just as I sprang from my saddle, a big Indian stepped from behind a post oak tree, and drew an arrow on me that looked as long as a barber's pole. I jumped behind another as spry as a city dry goods clerk when women come around shopping. I had no time to spare, for at that moment an arrow grazed my head so closely that it took the bark—a strip about the width of two of my fingers—from the tree. I drew a bead on him as he started to run, but that arrow had so unsettled my nerves that I missed him.

"The fight kept up pretty hot for about fifteen minutes, when the Indians retreated into the thick chaparral, leaving several of their warriors on the ground. I noticed my friend, Jeff Turner, several times during the fight. He was lifting a scalp from one of the Indians that he or someone else had slain. It is said that practice makes perfect. I was amazed to see how quickly the scalping was done and how quickly he reloaded his rifle to be ready for another. A slash and a jerk, and the scalp was soon dangling down from his belt. He never seemed to be in a hurry. He was cool and deliberate about everything he did as a carpenter about his work, when he is employed by the day and not the job.

"When the Indians began to retreat, one of them sprang upon one of our horses that was tied near the camp. He had forgotten, in his haste, to unfasten the rope. Round and round the tree he went until he had wound himself up to the body, just as Jeff Turner saw him and plugged him with a half-ounce ball, and had the Indian's scalp dangling from his belt before he was through kicking.

"After they had retreated to the chaparral, a little incident occurred that displayed the pluck of these red rascals when brought to bay. We were standing all huddled together, re-loading. We did not know but the Indians had retreated on purpose, to throw us off our guard. All at once, a keen yell and a report of a gun was heard. A tall chap named B——, who had come from the settlements, dropped his rifle and clasped his hands to his face, exclaiming, 'Boys, I am a dead man.' I looked around to see where the shot came from, and saw an Indian lying in the grass a little distance from us.

"His gun in his hand, the Indian was slowly sinking back into the grass, from which he had partly raised himself, by a dying effort, to take one last pop at the enemies of his race. I had seen this Indian fall in the fight, and supposed that he was dead, which he was in an instant after he had fired this last shot. I went to him at once and found that he was dead as a door nail, with his gun still tightly clasped in his hands. I found that seven rifle balls had entered his body. His wounds were plainly seen, for he had nothing on but his powderhorn and pouch.

"Our Indian hater came to him about the same time I did, and had his scalp in a jiffy. These scalps seemed to soothe the mind of Jeff Turner, as he told me they would. He soon became quite sociable after the fight, and once even laughed outright after hearing a story about shooting at a stump three times before the mistake was discovered. But the unnatural sound of his own voice seemed to frighten him, or maybe he had used up all the slack he had on hand, for I never saw him smile again.

"Luckily, B —— was worse scared than hurt, for the warrior's bullet had only grazed his head. He was standing near a blackjack tree, and the bark struck him in the face, causing him to think that the time had come for him to hand in his checks.

"The Indians had killed a fine buck, and the choice pieces were spitted before the fire. They were done to a turn. We had not eaten a bit all day, and seized upon this as the spoils of war. Together with some hard tack which we had brought along in our haversacks, we made a hearty supper. While eating, I could not help feeling sorry for the poor creatures that had prepared the venison about an hour before, and were now lying cold and stiff on the damp grass, soon be devoured by the vultures and wild animals.

"These reflections failed to take away my appetite, or if they did, a half dozen ribs and five pounds of meat disappeared with it. When we had finished our suppers, we changed our saddles from the horses we had been riding to those the Indians had stolen from us, which had been resting for some time. We took our back track to the settlements, where we arrived at about sun-up the next morning. We had ridden, during a part of a day and one night, about seventy-five miles, stopping only on the battleground.

"I never saw the Indian hater again. He left us for his camp on the Chicolite. I was told, when I was in the settlements several years afterwards, that he stayed around there for awhile, occasionally coming into the settlements for his supplies and ammunition. He always brought with him four or five Indian scalps. Finally, he disappeared. It is supposed that they at last caught him napping. At very least, Jeff Turner, the Indian hater, was never heard of after his last visit to the settlements."

Way back in the 1850s, the writer heard the old citizens relate stories of the Indian hater. Having now given the facts concerning the massacre of his family, and his subsequent life, as they were given by himself and those intimately associated with him, we can rest assured that the facts as related by Wallace are as near authentic as is possible to be obtained after the lapse of so many years. In presenting these facts, it is as reasonable and natural that we enter into sympathy with the parties taking upon themselves the burden of recovering this fair and beautiful land from the savages.

We can but regret, however, that these brave, noble men could not have been taught to leave the adjustment of these difficulties to Him who is to finally "judge the quick and the dead at His appearing," and who doeth all things well. Under the influence of that Book of books, they would not have been moved by the spirit of revenge. It matters not what troubles, trials and burdens we are called upon to bear in this life, if His Word is our guide we can trample them under our feet and abide the adjustment and restoration of all things. The being who presumes to take God's work into his hands is an object of supreme pity.

The historian delights in his work. His desire is to please the reader and, if facts are wanting, if he is not strictly scrupulous, he will supply. The same spirit prompts men to exaggerate hunting and fishing stories. The writer's natural desire is to please. With this prompting and with enthusiasm excited by the bravery of heroes, the imagination often carries us into unreasonable flights. It is only a strong man who can tell his own story in which he figures as the hero, and adhere strictly to the truth. Such narratives must be taken with some degree of allowance. They often go too far and bring upon themselves the odium of ridicule.

Anecdote of Tom Bird

At one time, in the town of Seymour, there was quite a number of guests seated at a dining table. Some of them were strangers who were in the country prospecting. They were listening to every word that was said. There were also at the table several cowboys who had been in the country but a short while, but who were trying to pass as pioneers in the presence of strangers. Several of us at the table had been in the country as many years as these young fellows had been in the world. They, however, ignored the fact and began telling of being on a certain Indian scout in which they had performed some wonderful feats. They even went so far as to give the place and date.

Tom Bird, a regular old Indian fighter, winked his eye at me (for he had but one eye—the Indians had shot out the other.) Tom smiled in a way to indicate that he knew they were lying, but he never said a word. Some parties present who knew Tom and me insisted upon us telling of some of our exploits. I declined. Tom did, as well, for a time. They continued to urge him. He reluctantly began by saying, "Several of you know there is a mountain down the river, near Fort Belknap, in Young County. You remember there is a valley between the mountains. The river and the valley are called Tonk Valley."

"Yes," said several present, "we know the place very well."

Tom continued, "This valley lies right along the river for about a mile in length. There is no crossing on the river, only at the end of the valley, and the mountain on the south is impassable." The party agreed again that they knew the place very well. "I went one morning across the river at the upper end of that valley. I was riding leisurely along, looking for my horses. There appeared right in front of me a large bunch of Indians that had just crossed the river a little below. I whirled my horse around as quickly as possible, in order to make the crossing I had just come over. There, to my utter amazement, another large body of Indians confronted me. I charged first one way and then another, until the Indians charged both ways, and run right up around me."

Tom stopped his story. One of the men who, in the beginning had been talking Indian, took the bait. "Well, Tom? What did they do?"

"Oh!" says Tom, "They killed me right there!"

Tom's illustrative story was to the point. It gave the parties present an idea of the value to be placed on stories told by those who relate secondhand history. Tom and I both knew that such a fight never took place where they said it did, for we both lived there at the time they said it took place. The pretend pioneers and Indian fighters felt the cut and realized how badly they had been sold out. In this narrative, what I state for facts I believe to be facts.

Schoolhouse Massacre

There are two very reliable parties in this, Knox County, who know all about this terrible massacre. It is not convenient to interview them, however, so I will give the account as related in Wilbarger's history. Its accuracy is vouched for. It was among the first depredations made by the Indians in daylight and was well reported at the time it occurred.

This massacre so intimidated the people that they would not send their children to school other than in the towns or where they were protected. Miss Ann Whitney was murdered at about 2 p.m. on Thursday, July 11, 1867. The place where this murder was committed was a small log schoolhouse in Hamilton County on the banks of the Leon River, in a beautiful valley about a mile and a half long, and three-quarters of a mile wide. This was called Warlene Valley.

The Howards lived one-half mile west and John Baggett lived a half mile east of the schoolhouse. Ezekiel Manning and Alexander Powers lived one and a half miles south and behind a high hill. The Massingills, Gauns, Stranglins, and Cal and James Kuykendall lived up the river within two miles. J. B. Hendrix and sons, Crockett and Abe, lived about two miles away. Judge D. C. Snow and Ned Livingston were three or four miles out. Pierson's ranch was six miles below. The town of Hamilton itself is located six miles south of the scene of this murder. This is a forcible instance of the cruel and fiendish barbarity practiced by this savage race in cold-blooded and cowardly murder.

This schoolhouse was built of unhewn logs, as was the custom in those days. The spaces between the logs were open, making it easier for the parties outside to fire upon the inmates during the attack. There was a small window on the north side, without a shutter. Olivia was the twelve year old daughter of John Barber, a stockman who lived northeast some ten or twelve miles. This daughter was boarding with some of the neighbors and attending school in the schoolhouse. Her father was expected to come by that week, while cow-hunting, to see her.

On the day and time John Alexander was expected by, a daughter of Alexander Powers was standing near the door on the south side of the building. From there, she saw a party of men on horseback rapidly approaching and recognized them as Indians. Miss Whitney, noticing her standing at the door gazing so intently, asked her what she saw. The girl replied that she saw persons coming toward the schoolhouse and she believed them to be Indians. Miss Whitney bade her take her seat saying, "Don't be foolish. They are cow hunters." She believed it was Mr. Barber and did not take the trouble to see for herself. Fatal error!

Mr. Powers' daughter was still uneasy. She looked out the door again and cried out, "They are Indians!" She grasped her little brother by the hand and made her escape through the window. This caused Miss Whitney to go to the door. She saw that Olivia was correct. She exclaimed, "They are Indians, and they're taking Mary!" Mary was a fine saddle animal, the property and pet of Miss Whitney. She had often made the remark, "If the Indians ever take Mary, they had best take me too."

Miss Whitney closed the door and bade the children to escape by the window, which they all did with the exception of Ezekiel Manning's daughter, Mary Jane, and two sons of James Kuykendall. Their teacher was very large and fleshy, weighing two hundred and thirty pounds. She could not get out of the window, nor hope to escape by running through the door. Many of the children crawled under the house and thus became unwilling witnesses to the tragedy that was enacted.

The Indians surrounded the house. One of them, who seemed to be the leader, said to Miss Whitney in pretty fair English, "Damn you! We've got you now!" She read her doom in the hideously painted faces and bloodthirsty manners of the savages. This heroic woman never lost her presence of mind. Desiring to save the lives of those under her care, she implored the Indian who had addressed her in English to take her life but to spare the children, if this would satisfy them. The savage held up three fingers. At this signal, they let their arrows fly, through the spaces between the logs of the schoolhouse. The arrows penetrated Miss Whitney's body.

Little Jane Manning clung to the skirts of her beloved teacher, whose lifeblood was gushing from her wounds. The garments of the fear-stricken child, as well as those of the children hiding beneath the floor, were stained with the blood of their devoted teacher. Such a scene as this should soften the hearts of obdurate savages or devils incarnate.

The Indians at last succeeded in breaking open the door. The fiends entered, but too late to inflict further pain upon Miss Whitney. Just as the brutes entered the threshold of her death prison, Miss Whitney's soul took its flight to be with the angels.

Upon perceiving that she was dead, the Indian who had first entered called to those outside. The one who spoke English came in. The Indian asked the Kuykendall boys if they wanted to go with them. Influenced by fear, one of them answered in the affirmative. The other declined. Strange to say, to the one who had answered no, they said, "Sit there," and placed the one who had said yes on a horse and took him with them. This was John Kuykendall. He was afterward purchased from them, after enduring for a long time unbearable torture. An Indian who had just about succeeded in getting Olivia Barber behind him on his horse was called into the house. In his absence, she made her escape. She was found by Josiah Massingill but the child was so wild with fear that she had to be run down on a horse the following day.

Miss Whitney was not scalped, nor were any of the children killed. Other things were going on in the vicinity which saved the lives of the children. Rest assured that their being spared was not the result of the pitiful pleadings of Miss Whitney. The savage knows no pity. About the time of the attack on the schoolhouse, two ladies rode into the valley from the south. They were Miss Amanda Howard and her sister-in-law, Mrs. Sarah Howard. They lived not far from the home of John Bagget—a bit further off and to the west.

Miss Amanda, who was an expert rider, was mounted on a young horse that she was breaking for her own use. Her sister-in-law was with her for assistance and company. They saw the Indians at the schoolhouse and, at first, took them to be cow hunters. They were discovered by the Indians before they had ridden very far up the valley. Two of the Indians started toward them. The ladies soon discovered their error and turned to reach Bagget's house. The Indians pursued closely.

Miss Amanda had considerable trouble in turning her horse. When she had gotten him into a good run, she looked back and into the gleaming eyes of one of the pursuers, who was now quickly gaining on her. Her horse took fright. She determined to make him leap Bagget's fence. The leap was a successful one and she reached Bagget's house in safety.

Mrs. Sarah Howard was not so successful. Her horse refused to leap the fence and, instead, went headlong over it. Her horse was caught by the Indian pursuing her. She recovered in an instant and made her escape to the house, as the Indian was not able to manage capturing both horse and rider. In the east end of the valley, at the same time, an immigrant was traveling about halfway across. The Indians attacked and killed him, but did not scalp him, nor did they molest his wife and children who were in the wagon.

The brave and heroic Miss Howard, realizing that the lives of people of the valley were in imminent danger, determined, at the risk of her own life, to save them. The scheme was a bold one, and rightly deserves a place in the annals of heroic deeds. In order for her to accomplish her purpose, she was compelled to ride obliquely toward the Indians and to outride them, in order to make the crossing over the high hill. This was her only route to the lower settlements.

Her plans fully matured, Miss Howard again mounted her half-broken steed. Unheeding fences, she reached the valley and began that perilous ride to the hill. The Indians saw her and at once read her design. The Indians were aware that if people in the settlements knew about their raids in the valley, they would be instantly pursued. Raising the usual keen Indian yell, and joined by the Indians who were at the schoolhouse, the race began. They rushed pell-mell to cut her off from the crossing.

Picture, if you can, this scene: Miss Whitney pierced with scores of arrows, her pupils crazed with fright, expecting at any moment to be stung with an arrow or captured; Miss Howard on this unbroken horse, riding, as it were, into the very jaws of death, to notify the settlers of their danger. The writer challenges the world for the presentation of a little scene more thrilling than this one.

The arrows whistled around Miss Howard, but she ascended the hill in safety. The Indians at once left the schoolhouse in the valley, taking the little Kuykendall boy with them. The lives of many of the worthy pioneers were saved by the intrepid bravery of this girl, only seventeen years of age. On she rode from house to house, stopping just long enough at each place to tell the sad story.

She first reached the Hendrix ranch. Mr. Hendrix at once sent his son to Pierson's ranch to secure the blood hounds. Miss Howard continued to Judge Snow's. The men were away, but Miss Belle Snow mounted a horse and warned those south of there. When young Abe Hendrix reached Pierson's ranch, the oldest Pierson son in company with Chap and Volney Howard, brothers of Miss Amanda, were out hunting. They did not return until it was nearly night and the day had been lost. When they returned, they and their horses were tired, but when they heard the startling news, or as much of it as was then known—they supposed that all at the schoolhouse and in the immigrants' wagon had been murdered—with a goodbye to homefolks, Pierson blew his horn. The hounds quickly responded.

Pierson, with the Howards and Abe Hendrix, rode rapidly away. They collected as many as seven men and then, going to Manning's place, they got the course the raiders had taken. It was eleven o'clock at night before they were well on the trail, for the Indians seemed to have scattered. The night was sultry and hot. At the west end of the prairie, where the Indians went out, it was both brushy and rocky. It was difficult for the dogs to keep the trail. There was no water in the direction they went until they got to Cow House Creek. The dogs could hardly be induced to leave the water until they were thoroughly cooled. Both riders and horses were suffering, but no time was to be lost. They wished to overtake the enemy before they reached the mountains.

The Indians were too far in advance. The pursuers, when they at length reached the mountains, found them densely covered with chaparral and rocks. It was almost impossible for them to get through. One man's horse had given out and the dogs couldn't be urged any further. The party sent him with the dogs to water, while they continued the chase until night stopped them. They had now ridden about one hundred miles without taking any rest. This band of Indians were well-mounted. They had abandoned all the horses they were driving and aimed now only to escape.

The Kuykendall boy said he saw his friends in pursuit at about sunrise, then the Indians took to the chaparral. One Indian lead the horse to which the boy was tied, and he was not permitted by his captors to dismount for the next two days and nights. When he did, the skin was peeled from his legs. The Indians were about six miles ahead when the white men abandoned the chase.

Salt Creek Massacre

In 1874, Colonel Mackenzie of the United States Army succeeded in forcing the Comanches onto the reservation in the Indian Territory, but not until he had strategically succeeded in getting possession of their horses. The horses were killed and the Indians were left afoot, and their arms were taken from them for a time. After being fed by the United States and drawing annual rent on their lands, they are now behaving well and some are even making money. Too much cannot be said in praise of the noble Mackenzie who, by true and faithful discharge of his duty, gave our whole frontier relief from those cruel Indian raids. We owe him a lasting debt of gratitude that I often wish we had a more sustainable way of expressing.

Early in the spring of 1870, Captain Julian Fields, of Mansfield in Tarrant County, fitted out one of the finest mule trains I ever saw. The mules were purchased in Missouri late in the previous fall when Captain Fields, my brother and others were up there with cattle for market. They were in fine condition, and the wagons and harnesses were new and of the best quality. There were six teams of six mules each and they represented a considerable sum of money. Fields and R. A. Mann had a government contract to supply the post at Fort Griffin with both flour and grain. They could use their teams the greater part of the time in filling this contract, and the remainder of the time they expected to use the teams in hauling for others.

With a fine set of teamsters, well armed and otherwise equipped, they started from Jacksboro in Jack County, loaded with flour, for Fort Griffin in Shackelford County. When they reached a point on Salt Creek prairie, nine miles from the present town of Graham, they were attacked by about one hundred and fifty Kiowa Indians, led by their chiefs Satanta, Satank and Big Tree. I suppose these were three of the most bloodthirsty villains that ever raided on our frontier.

There were two men with each mule team, making twelve in all, and if memory serves me right, the entire train was in the charge of a man named Long. Late in the evening, as the train was crossing a smooth prairie ridge, this large force of Indians made their attack. The teamsters arranged their wagons in a circle as quickly as possible, so as to protect themselves from the shots of the enemy. Being overwhelmingly outnumbered by the Indians, the teamsters were able to repulse them for only a short time. Only two made their escape to report the terrible massacre to the commander at Fort Richardson, near Jacksboro. One man, who was wounded in the battle, was tied to the wheel of one of the wagons and burned to death while the train was being destroyed by fire.

Fortunately for the settlers, at this time, General W. T. Sherman was making a tour of inspection of all frontier posts and, not many hours before this terrible massacre, had passed over the very same road. This was during those dark Reconstruction days of the South when our appeals for protection by the general government were being passed wholly unheard and unheeded. It was fortunate that General Sherman so narrowly escaped, for he would no doubt have shared a similar fate to that of the teamsters if he had only been by a few hours later. He therefore could see and understand plainly, from nearly a personal experience, the real condition of our defenseless and suffering people, against whom the party then in power held prejudice on account of the Civil War. Now, one of the great leaders of the North during that war—one high in authority, honest and capable as a leader—was present near the place where he could see and feel the full force of this outrage to civilization. Seeing this fine train, engaged in hauling supplies to the government post, destroyed and the men cruelly murdered, Sherman could the more easily understand and appreciate the importance of rendering protection.

The effect was to change the whole line of policy in handling these murderers and thieves. General Sherman was at or near Fort Richardson when the men who had escaped the massacre reached home with the report. He sent Colonel Mackenzie immediately out to the place to learn all of the facts concerning the incident. Upon his return, Colonel Mackenzie reported that the account given by the men from the train was correct in every particular.

General Sherman remained at Fort Richardson for one day and there met a committee of representative men from among the best citizens of the country. Among them were W. W. Duke, R. J. Winters, Judge J. R. Robinson, W. M. McConnell (a former Union soldier), Peter Hart and General H. H. Gaines. These gentlemen presented to General Sherman the exact condition of affairs on the frontier, showing how treacherous and unworthy the Indians were of the kind of treatment they were receiving at the time from the government. They showed him, too, that those who were suffering most were those who took no part nor interest in politics, but were innocent and defenseless women and children and, as in this instance, men who were in the employ of the government. General Sherman gave this committee very close attention and on the next day, the 19th of May, he went on to Fort Sill in the Indian Territory. He arrived there on the 21st and remained for some time.

About the 27th, as shown by a diary kept by Colonel Smythe, and quoted in Wilbarger's history of Indian depredations, a number of Indian chiefs came into the agency at Fort Sill to draw rations from the government. Among them were Satanta, Satank, Kicking Bird, Lone Wolf and others. While talking with the agent, Tatum, Satanta told him that he had been in a big fight, had killed a lot of teamsters and had brought in forty-one fine mules. He said that he was in command and made the fight, and that if anyone else claimed the honor, they were liars. He pointed at Satank and Big Tree as being present, but under his command.

Agent Tatum immediately reported this to General Sherman and requested that these chiefs should be punished. Whereupon, General Sherman sent for them, and old Satanta acknowledged the facts reported to the General. But when General Sherman informed the chiefs that he would put them in confinement and send them to Texas to be tried for the crime, Satanta realized the situation he was in and began to evade the truth. He said that he was present in the fight but did not kill anyone or take any active part in the fight in any way. He stated that some of his young men wanted to go on a raid and that he just went along to show them how to fight. Satanta said, too, that the white people had killed and wounded a lot of his people, but this would now put him right, and that he would now stop doing any more harm. He wanted to forget the past and begin anew.

The General told the chief how cowardly he thought it was for one hundred and fifty warriors to kill twelve teamsters, but that if Satanta desired a battle, that his soldiers were very ready at any time to engage with them. After being told by the General that he, with Satank and Big Tree would be sent to Texas to be tried, Satanta said he would prefer to be shot.

When Kicking Bird arose, he said that he had done all in his power to keep his young men from going to Texas to plunder, as General Grierson and his agent well knew. He asked General Sherman to release his friend Satanta and said that he would restore all the mules that they had captured. General Sherman said that he appreciated Kicking Bird's good behavior, and that he would be well treated as long as he continued to behave, but that the other men would be sent to Texas for trial.

About twenty armed soldiers came up in front of the building where this council was being held, and the Indians were very much excited. Nearly every Indian had a rifle and a Colt revolver. Old Kicking Bird continued his efforts to secure the release of the chief who had been arrested. He claimed to be friendly to the whites and would be sorry if war were the result of this affair but that if it was, he would stay with his people.

Now Lone Wolf came up with a rifle, sixshooter, and bows and arrows. He gave the bow and arrows to one Indian who was unarmed and the sixshooter to another. The Indian with the bow at once strung it and took from the quiver a handful of arrows, while Lone Wolf seated himself and cocked his rifle. Thereupon, the soldiers made ready to fire upon the crowd, but Satanta and some of the others threw up their hands, crying, "No shoot! No shoot!" The soldiers were then commanded to hold their fire. Just at this moment, firing was heard outside of the fort, the result of an order to let no Indian pass without further instructions. Some, attempting to pass and being halted, shot the sentinel with an arrow. Immediately, the Indian who had shot the arrow was then shot and killed by the sentinel.

When the excitement had subsided to some extent, General Sherman commanded the Indians to bring in the mules, which Kicking Bird agreed to do. When he went out after them, he discovered that the squaws had taken fright and left with all their animals, except eight, which were taken into the possession of the soldiers. All the Indians were then allowed to leave except for the prisoners, who were placed in irons and very closely guarded. Afterwards, under a strong guard commanded by Colonel Mackenzie, they were transferred to the jail at Jacksboro.

On the way to Jacksboro, Satank actually gnawed the flesh from his arms, attempting to free himself from the shackles. He was discovered in the act of attempting to kill one of the soldiers and was shot dead on the spot. The death of Satank seemed to cause great fear among the other chiefs, so the soldiers had no trouble with the other prisoners, who were placed safely in the jail at Jacksboro and kept in chains until their trial.

It seemed at the time almost providential that General Sherman's visit should occur just as these transactions were occurring, and that these cruel, bloody-handed fiends in human form were detected by him in person, as it were, in the very act of perpetrating one of the most inhuman crimes; that they, through the influence of Colonel Mackenzie and the Indian agent, Tatum, should be brought to justice by being placed in close confinement, and their terrible, fiendish work brought abruptly to a close. A sigh of relief seemed to pass along our whole frontier. The happiness of everyone was brightened and they esteemed life more dearly. They even began to appreciate their homes and property to a higher degree than ever before, which was apparent from the improvements that were started soon after.

Although the Indians came several times after the arrests and the death of Satank, they were quite different and were never so bold again as to venture far into the settlements. They began to realize that they could not resist the influx of inhabitants into western Texas, and that soon it would be the home of the white man instead of their once happy hunting ground. The influence of General Sherman was in favor of the frontier throughout the United States, and his honest, straightforward course checked the expressions of sympathy that were being made by the Northern and Eastern people toward the oppressed Indian, which had only added encouragement to their efforts of robbery and fiendish murder in these sparsely settled counties. Everyone rejoiced that at last the chiefs were prisoners and were to face the courts in a fair trial for their heinous crimes.

Judge Charles Soward, in whose district the crimes were committed and under whose jurisdiction the cases were to be tried, came to Jacksboro the following July, and the time was set for the trial of the cases against the chiefs. S. W. T. Lanham appeared for the government, as the prosecuting attorney. Thomas Ball of Jacksboro and a gentleman named Woolfork, of Weatherford, appeared as attorneys for the defense, both being very able lawyers. Twelve of the very best men of the country were selected as jurors. One of the teamsters who escaped the massacre, Tom Brazeal, Agent Tatum and General Grierson of the United States Army were the principal witnesses for the State.

During the trial, the prisoners were taken to and from the jail by a strong military guard which remained present during the whole progress of the trial, both for the protection of the civil authorities as well as the protection of the prisoners at the bar. A special effort was made by all those who were participants in the trial, as well as by those who were only spectators, to make sure that civil law was properly enforced. Great care was taken by all to ensure that the prisoners should have a fair and impartial trial before the courts of the country.

I will here give the names of the jurors in this case, as found in Wilbarger's history: T. W. Williams, John Cameron, Everett Johnson, H. B. Verner, Stanley Cooper, William Hensely, J. H. Brown, Peyton Lynn, Peter Hart, Daniel Brown, L. P. Bunch and James Cooley. I was personally acquainted with nearly all of these jurors, having lived in Jack County among them for quite a number of years. I know that they were well qualified in every particular for this important service, being men above the medium for intelligence and honor. Although I was in and around Jack County during the trial, I hesitate to attempt to give the particulars of so important an event solely from memory and will, therefore, quote the proceedings of the court from Wilbarger's history, as they were taken directly from the court records.

"In taking the testimony, the witnesses were very closely questioned and cross-questioned, and the attorneys for the defense took all the pains that could have been taken in defending a white man being tried under a similar charge. The attorneys for the defense both made very able speeches, presenting every phase of the case that could in any way mollify the crime or give reason to cause doubt of their guilt. Then S. W. T. Lanham, one of the best of men and one of superior ability at that time, closed the trial with a strong, logical speech in which he showed a perfect chain of testimony and that from very reliable witnesses who were not only men of prominence, but were men of the strictest integrity. He then asked for a verdict in accordance with the law and the evidence.

"Then old Satanta was permitted to speak, which he did partly by signs and partly by words. Raising his hands with the handcuffs on them, he said, 'I cannot speak with these things upon my wrists like I am a squaw. Has anything been heard from the great Father? I have never been so near Tehanna (Texas) before. I look around me. I see your braves, squaws and papooses. I have said in my heart that I will get back to my people. I will never make war upon you. I have always been a friend to the white man ever since I was so high (pointing to a boy in the courtroom.) My tribe have taunted me and have called me a squaw because I have been the friend of the Tehanna. I am suffering now for the crimes of bad Indians—of Satank, Lone Wolf, Kicking Bird, Big Bow, Eagle Heart—and if you will let me, I will go kill the last three with my own hand. I did not kill the Tehanna. I came down Pease River as a big medicine man, to doctor the braves. I am a big chief among people, and have a great influence among the warriors of my tribe. They know my voice and hear my words. If you will let me go back to my people, I will withdraw my warriors from Tehanna. I will take them all across the Red River and that shall be the line between us and the pale face. I will wash out the spots of blood and make it a white land, and the Tehanna may plow and drive their oxen to the banks of the Red River. But if you kill me, it will be like a spark in the prairie, making big fire burn heap.'

"The jury was out only a short time and returned a verdict of guilty of murder in the first degree, and fixed his punishment at death. The whole audience gave long and loud expressions of approval at the verdict. This closed a trial of the greatest importance to Texas, as well as to the whole country, that has ever occurred in any Texas court, for on it hinged the destiny of our frontier people, their homes and their future happiness.

"No one properly understands, except from actual experience, the horrors of being in a continual dread of such as was threatened to the people of the frontier by these savage raids. They far exceeded the horrors of any other war from the brutality with which these beings, clothed with the intelligence of the human, yet controlled only by the brutal instincts of the beast, could inflict death or punishment upon their captives. Having been reared to look upon life as only one of self-preservation, the Indians found no greater joy than the torture of their enemies, nor could any appeal be made by that enemy to their sympathy or mercy. They were absolute strangers to anything like an affection for others, especially for the white man, and nothing delighted them more than the torture of their captives, and the greatest suffering furnished this brutal race with its greatest delight.

"After the verdict, the prisoners were duly sentenced by the court to be hung on the first day of the following September, in 1871. Tatum, the Indian agent at Fort Sill, wrote a letter to General Sherman in which he said: 'Permit me to urge, independent of my conscientious scruples against capital punishment, that as a matter of policy, it would be best for the inhabitants of Texas, that Satanta and Big Tree be not executed for some time, if at all, for reason that, if they are kept as prisoners, the Indians will have hope to have them released, which will be a restraining influence upon their actions. If they are executed, the Indians will be very likely to seek revenge by the wholesale slaughter of white people.'

"Tatum also wrote to District Attorney Lanham the following letter: 'In view of the trial of Satanta and Big Tree, Kiowa chiefs, of this agency, permit me to remind you that the two characteristic traits of Indians are a fondness for revenge and a dread of confinement. From my knowledge of them, I believe that if the prisoners should be convicted of murder, it would be a more severe punishment to them to confine them for life than to execute them, and imprisonment would probably save the lives of some of the white people. If they be executed, it is more than probable that some of the other Kiowas would seek revenge in the murder of some white citizens. This is my judgment, from a policy standpoint. But if we judge it from a Christian standpoint, I believe we should in all cases, even of murder in the first degree, confine person for life, and leave to God his prerogative to determine when a person has lived long enough.'

"Judge Charles Soward, who presided as judge in the trial, also recommended commutation of the sentence, as follows: 'Weatherford, Parker County, Texas, July 10th 1871. Governor E. J. Davis: Sir—I have, your honor, to say that the last term is regarded as of more interest to our frontier than any court that has ever been held in the State. Upon arriving at Jacksboro, we dispatched a posse of five citizens to Fort Sill for the necessary witnesses, and through the assistance of Colonel Mackenzie, commanding United States Army at Fort Richardson, General Grierson, commander at Fort Sill, and Lowrie Tatum, Indian agent, we obtained the necessary witnesses for the State. After a fair and impartial trial, with the defendants having the best counsel at the command of the court, the jury returned a verdict of murder in the first degree and fixed the punishment at death. Mr. Tatum expresses a strong desire that they should be punished by imprisonment for life, but the jury thought differently.

"'I passed sentence upon them on the 8th of July, and fixed the time of their execution at Friday, September first next. I must say here that I concur with Mr. Tatum as to the punishment, simply, however, upon a political view of the matter. Mr. Tatum has indicated that if they be tried, convicted and imprisoned as punishment, that he would render all the assistance in his power to the civil authorities in bringing others of those tribes on the reservations, who have been guilty of outrages in Texas, for trial and just punishment. I would have petitioned your excellency to commute their punishment to imprisonment for life, were it not that I know that a great majority of the people of the frontier demand their execution. Your excellency, however, acting for the weal of the State at large, and free from the passions of the masses, may see fit to commute their punishment. If so, I say amen!

"'Now, while entertaining the opinion that the present policy of the United States toward these wild tribes is founded on supreme folly, nevertheless, I see in this new phase of the Quaker policy, which culminated in the trial and conviction of the great chief, Satanta, and the brave, Big Tree, by civil authority, a solution of our difficulties. And if we will utilize our vantage ground, I think we will speedily redeem our borders from the ravages of the reservation Indians.

"'During the trial of Satanta and Big Tree, it appeared from legitimate testimony that Big Bow, Fast Bear and Eagle Heart were in the last raid, that resulted in the murder of seven men and the capture of forty-one head of fine mules. Now, I most earnestly request your excellency to issue your requisition for the above named Indians to be turned over to the sheriff of Jack County. You will please send your commission through General Reynolds to Colonel Mackenzie at Fort Richardson. Colonel Mackenzie informs me that he is ready and will execute the commission. Tatum, the agent, is under promise to render all the assistance in his power.

"Wish many wishes for your good health, I remain, with much respect, your obedient servant, Charles Soward, Judge. Thirteenth Judicial District, Texas.'

"Governor Davis responded thusly: 'Dear Sir—Your communication of the tenth ult. has been received, recommending the commutation of the sentence in the case of Satanta and Big Tree. I have thought your recommendation a good one, and have accordingly directed that the sentence of these Indians be commuted to imprisonment for life. - Respectfully, Edm'd J. Davis, Governor.'

"Governor Davis, on August 2nd, issued the following proclamation, officially commuting the sentences of Satanta and Big Tree to imprisonment for life: 'STATE OF TEXAS: To All Whom These Presents Shall Come—Whereas, at the July term, A. D. 1871, of the District Court of Jack County, in said State, one Satanta and Big Tree, known as Indians of the Kiowa tribe, were tried and convicted on a charge of murder, and sentenced therefor to suffer the death penalty, on the first day of September, A. D. 1871, and whereas, it is deemed that a commutation of said sentence to imprisonment for life will be more likely to operate as a restraint upon others of the tribe to which these Indians belong, and whereas, the killing for which these Indians were sentenced can hardly be considered as a just consideration of the animus as coming within the technical crime of murder, under the statutes of the State, but rather as an act of savage warfare: Now, therefore, I, Edmund J. Davis, Governor of Texas, by virtue of the authority vested in me by the constitution of the State, do hereby commute the sentence of Satanta and Big Tree to imprisonment for life at hard labor in the State penitentiary, and hereby direct the clerk of the District Court of Jack County to make this commutation of sentence a matter of record in his office.'"

H. C. Woods, by command of Major General Reynolds, issued a special order that Satanta and Big Tree were to be delivered under suitable guard to the warden of the penitentiary at Huntsville. Special instructions were given in the order that, to ensure the safety of the prisoners en route, all communication of the prisoners with civilians was to be carefully prevented and strictly forbidden. The forty-one mules were never returned to their owners, but ten or twelve years after they were taken by the Indians, by a special act of Congress, the government gave Captain Fields a very good remuneration for the destruction of his train by its red pets.

I well remember how everyone who had been living about us in such terrific dread, when the Comanches and Kiowas were moved to the reservation, took new courage, and ranch property soon doubled and trebled in value. People who had abandoned their homes soon returned to them, and in the short space of a few years, a wave of prosperity swept all along our whole frontier. Those who had borne with such patience and fortitude the privations and trials of this terrible ordeal felt most its invigorating influence. Many of them became wealthy from the enhancement of the values of their property and are today living in comfort and enjoying the peace and pleasures purchased by their own suffering.

Now, all we can do for them is give them credit for what they did, and cherish their memory in a way that will show our gratitude and perpetuate their names among the honored of the land. One object I have in writing these lines (and this I hope to attain to some extent by the help of others) is to commit to record the heroic deeds of some whom I have known well, and of whose suffering I had a personal knowledge, and who are now sleeping in unmarked and unknown graves.

Before we begin the story of another of these great tragedies, I will say that I have conversed with several different parties who had a personal knowledge of certain interesting events which occurred back in those dark days, and I find how treacherous and unreliable is human memory; for their memories not only differ from mine, but each differs from the others concerning the things that ought to be remembered distinctly by us all alike. When this is the case, it is difficult for the narrator to determine just what is the truth. As an illustration of the differences that occur in the memory of those events, I will relate the following:

Just before the close of the Civil War, there lived on Deep Creek, in Wise County, in a beautiful valley surrounded by timber, an old Doctor Bowman, who had somehow succeeded in keeping, all through these troublesome times, a nice bunch of horses without ever having lost any. He worked his own farm, and his daughter, Sallie Bowman, watched and kept the horses. When it was high moon and the Indians were liable to be in the neighborhood, she kept the horses hidden in this valley as best she could in the brush. When there was no danger of their being around, she ventured out on the high prairie with them, but always at the least intimation of danger, she would rush them immediately to the valley and hide them in the brush.

The doctor was very generally out among the people, but if there was any sign of Indians, he at once made his way home and posted Sallie in regard to the fact. At a time when the Indians were least expected, she was with the horses out upon the high land. She was mounted upon her finest horse, a stallion, feeling reasonably secure but no doubt watching for danger, as she had always been accustomed to do at all times. There was at the time a bunch of Indians coming up the creek on the other side of the ridge on which she had her horses. She soon saw some of the horses which they were driving, and at once undertook to drive hers into the valley near her home. But her horses, catching sight of the Indians' horses, became somewhat hard to manage. About this time, the Indians saw her and, surmising what she was attempting to do, immediately began to cut her off from her home.

Seeing that not only her horse but she herself was in danger, at last sought to save herself by flight to the timber. The Indians ran obliquely across the timber and reached the valley just as she did. They chased her up to within full view of home, crowded around her, killed and scalped her, in plain sight of the balance of the family. Her father had just arrived to give her notice of the danger and was powerless to assist her against such numbers.

Now, some of our old neighbors say that she was killed in the timber before she reached the open valley in sight of home and friends. So I find that when one is compelled to rely upon memory alone, after the lapse of some years, great caution should be exercised in order to state the exact truth, and yet no more than the truth.

Dillard Brothers' Fight with the Indians

In 1872, Henry and Willie Dillard had a fight with the Indians and narrowly escaped death. I obtained my information of this fight from William Dillard, one of the participants, who now resides at Benjamin, Texas, and the statement of Major Graham of Graham, Texas, as found in Wilbarger's *Indian Depredations in Texas*, published in 1888. I knew Major Graham personally and know that he was perfectly reliable, and from my acquaintance with Mr. Dillard, my neighbor, feel the same way toward him. Both reports correspond perfectly.

Major Graham brought Henry Dillard with him from Kentucky in 1869. From then until 1872, Henry resided in and around the town of Graham. Fort Griffin was then a government post, with a garrison of soldiers, and proved a good market for the sale of produce. Dillard planted a crop on a farm near old Fort Belknap, where he lived almost alone. He became so lonesome that he wrote his brother in Kentucky to come and live with him. In the fall of 1872, Willie Dillard, a stout and active boy of eleven years, landed in Texas on his brother's farm. Henry was a very energetic boy, about twenty years of age.

Among the other things raised on the Dillard farm that fall was a fine crop of watermelons, which Henry concluded to market at Fort Griffin. He and Willie loaded their wagon and, after arming themselves with a gun and sixshooter, started out. At Fort Griffin they found a ready sale. On their return, Henry was lying in the wagon bed asleep, and Willie was driving the team. When they had gone some distance in this way, Willie saw ahead of them about thirty Indians in warpaint, well armed and well mounted. He screamed to his sleeping brother, "Look at the Indians!" Henry seized the gun and sixshooter and, springing out of the wagon, he made for the timber, calling for Willie to follow. It was about one hundred and fifty yards to this shelter, and the Indians at once charged in an effort to kill them before they reached protection.

Henry made a shot with his Winchester, which served to stop the Indians, but no damage was done and they made another charge. He shot a second time with like effect. Undaunted came the Indians and Henry, remembering Major Graham's instructions to shoot low in fighting Indians to get below their shields, by a third shot killed not only a rider but his horse, as well. The Indians were firing all the while but as it was a fight on the run, Henry and Willie were unharmed. From this point on, Henry made every shot count while Willie loaded the guns. Before they could reach the timber, the Indians made another desperate effort to cut them off. An old warrior charged right up to Willie, who screamed to his brother that they were about to get him, and Henry commanded him to shoot. Just as the Indian was in the act of grabbing Willie, he threw his pistol quite nearly against the Indian and fired. Off rolled the Indian, dead at his feet.

The Indians checked, and the Dillard boys reached the timber safely. The Indians did not care to renew the engagement and, immediately withdrawing, moved off to Fort Sill. There they reported having had a fight with a big captain and a little boy, but the captain's medicine was too strong for them. Henry and Willie, after nightfall, went to a ranch where they procured horses and, returning to Fort Griffin, they reported the events to the commander who sent out a detachment of troops. The troops took the trail of the Indians and followed it for two days. Returning, they reported that they found where the Indians had camped, and that a number of their grass beds were covered with blood.

KILLING AND SCALPING OF NICK DAWSON

The counties of Montague, Wise, Jack, Young, Parker and Palo Pinto are peculiarly situated in that country known as the Upper Cross Timbers, being partly timbered and partly prairie. In the brush and timber the Indians could skulk and hide during the day, and at night they could prowl through the country, steal horses, and kill and scalp people. These were, at the beginning of the Civil War, the border counties, and were at the time rather in a defenseless condition since both men and arms were carried away to be used in the Confederate service. While in none of the histories of those days is found anything much concerning Wise County, it is a fact that the people of that county suffered as much from the ravages of Indians, if not more, than did those of any other county.

I have already given one instance, from the early days, of the scalping of Josiah Wilbarger, where one of his friends had a strong presentiment that lead to his rescue. I want now to give another, occurring a few years after the Civil War, in Wise County, which was almost as strange as the one referred to above.

Nick Dawson was a man of great courage, and one who was always ready, when the opportunity offered, to fight the dreaded Comanche. His body was at that time already marked by the scars of battle made by the Indians. Although Indian blood, to some extent, coursed in his veins, he was and had been for some time an honorable citizen of Wise County. He lived in the southeastern part, on the high prairie and close to the main passway used by the Indians when they made a raid in that part of the country. His mother was a widow with several children, who Nick had helped to support and raise. At the time of his death, he had a family of his own, and had living with him a Choctaw Indian boy who quite nearly worshipped him and called him Uncle Nick.

Nick was out one day riding a fine racehorse and hunting a valuable mare he had running on the open range.

While on the search for this animal, he stopped at Captain Jerry Burnett's ranch. There, on the back gallery of the residence, Nick reached up and wrote on the wall his name and post office address. In talking with T. H. Burnett, a son of Captain Burnett, I learned that his father would never let that name be erased as long as that house stood, for those were the last words that Nick ever wrote.

After eating his dinner, he returned to the range in search of the mare. He had perhaps found her and tied her to the tail of the horse he was riding, as was thought afterwards. Nick was out on the head of Morris' branch amid a considerable bunch of thick timber and briers in a low valley, where no one could be seen for any great distance. A band of Indians, evidently concealing themselves there waiting for nightfall to make a raid over the high prairie, saw him there. Dawson either mistook them for stockmen and approached them, or he ended up near them quite by accident. They at once pursued him over a high prairie divide for two or three miles before they succeeded in overtaking him. They killed and scalped him and then, in a manner too horrible to be related here, they mutilated his body. Oddly enough, though, they did not remove his five-shooter from his body.

That night, his failure to reach home, although it was a common occurrence with him, caused his family some uneasiness since they'd heard a band of Indians had been in the neighborhood. In the night, the Choctaw boy sprang up from his bed, exclaiming, "Uncle Nick is killed and the Indians have scalped him!" The family thought nothing of it until he was asleep again, saw the same scene and just could not be consoled about it anymore. The next day, a search was made and Nick was found in just the condition described by the Choctaw boy. Just how and why these visions are presented, we cannot tell, for they lie out of and beyond our comprehension. Nevertheless, they are true.

When Nick Dawson was found, fifteen or twenty men followed the trail of the Indians. They had about one hundred and fifty horses that they had stolen on the night after the killing of Dawson. In talking today with Colonel P. C. Sams, I was reminded that while this party of men was not a great distance behind the Indians, another party from the Mose Ball settlement on Black Creek waylaid the trail that the Indians usually went back on. When the savages ran into this ambuscade formed for them, they at once took fright and scattered in different directions. In this way, they made their escape but left behind all of the stolen stock, which afterwards was returned to the proper owners.

Among the horses captured from the Indians was the fine horse that Nick Dawson was riding at the time of his death. The brings me to the reason for my mention that it was believed that Nick, at the time of his death, had his mare tied to the tail of his horse for the purpose of leading her. When the horse was recaptured, a good part of its tail was pulled out, and when the mare was recovered, she had a piece of rope upon her neck. This largely accounts for the Indians being able to overtake Nick Dawson. There was, however, a peculiarity in the race he made—he ran in a zig-zag way that those who knew him could not account for his doing. He well knew the mode of pursuit that the Comanches used. He knew that they would, in pursuit, spread out so as to cover a considerable amount of ground, so that in the event any one of their number should be obstructed in any way, then some other one of their number could avoid the same and continue the chase. In the race with Dawson, it worked well, for they were able to cut off every curve made by him, as was clear to those who traced the course of the chase in the tracks that the horses left on the ground.

It is useless to call attention to the fact that those dangerous times offered to the worst class of men the opportunity to commit crimes of theft and robbery, and then let the Indians bear the blame therefor. Some of those who are familiar with the story of Nick Dawson have thought that this was one of those instances, and that it might have been the act of a clan of thieves who had been chased off

previously by Nick Dawson and others. It was said at that
time that some of the thieves had been caught but never
brought back; or, in other words, that they had been disposed of where they were found. Of course, all of this is
speculation. It was thought by people in general at that
time that it was not safe for white people to go about the
thickets and brush in the daytime, or to be on the prairie
at night, especially during a full moon. The Indians were
accustomed to secret themselves in the brush during the
day, and to come out on the prairie during the night to do
their stealing.

I still remember well those gloomy, dismal feelings that
would possess us all during those bright moonshiny nights,
which may sound so lovely to the reader. The dread of danger would invariably present itself to one's mind and, so
forcibly, that it was impossible to shake it off. Sometimes,
even now, such nights still bring back for a moment a taste
of the same kind of fear of impending evil, although now,
in my old age, I have again learned to love those beautiful
nights as I did in my boyhood days.

About the time that Nick Dawson was killed, a party of
Indians which had been defeated and their horses stolen
from them, as was done in the Dawson case, were going
back west with all their speed. I do not believe, as some of
our neighbors do, that this was the same gang that killed
Dawson. They were passing the house of old man Hamp-
ton when his son, about sixteen or eighteen years old, was
at the woodpile, chopping wood. The boy was deaf and
dumb. He was not conscious of the Indians' approach and
made no effort to escape. In passing, one of them threw a
lariat over his neck. They dragged him for a mile through
the brush and rocks, literally tearing his body to pieces. I
am sorry that I am not able to give a more detailed account
of this sad occurrence, but memory fails me.

Massacre of Camerons and Masons

In reviewing the killing of Nick Dawson, and the opinion of some of the neighbors at the time that it was instigated by bad white men, I am forcibly reminded of a very sad occurrence which happened on Cameron's Creek in Lost Valley, one of the most picturesque places that I have ever seen. The broad, beautiful prairie valley, surrounded on every side by high, rolling, timbered hills and mountains, gives a happy contrast to the scenery that is simply sublime. The days of danger were not yet passed when I first saw this valley and roamed over these hills, for it was just after the destruction of Captain Warren's fine mule train, which occurred in the extreme southern part of this valley.

At the time that Captain J. C. Loving, that noble and generous man, was ranching in Lost Valley on Cameron's Creek, I was ranching near him on the north and was in almost daily communication with him. We frequently talked over the many thrilling events that had, in days gone by, transpired there, along with others of the earliest settlers of this part of the country such as Bud Willet, Car. Hunt and Pat Sweeney. Here I received the first account that I ever had of the massacre of the Camerons and Masons.

Mr. Cameron had been in Texas for some years when he settled on Cameron's Creek in Lost Valley, near its edge, in 1859. Mr. Mason settled and built his house not far from Cameron's. I was then living seventy-five or eighty miles east of them, but several of my neighbors had settled but a few miles from them and know all of the particulars of their being killed. It seems that after being in the country for some time without having been molested by the Indians, Cameron and Mason became careless about carrying arms with them at all times, and this fact accounts for the murder of their families.

In the spring of 1859, Cameron and his sixteen year old boy went to the field to work, leaving their guns at the house. And while busy at work and before they were aware of an Indian presence, the savages surrounded them. In the attempt to escape to the house, they were both killed. Mrs. Cameron instinctively started out to meet them, but seeing that they were both being killed, attempted to hide with her two year old baby in the cow lot. Unfortunately, she was discovered by the Indians, who rushed to her place of concealment. They killed her with an axe, but left her baby unharmed by her side. Another son of Mr. Cameron started for Mr. Mason's and would perhaps have reached there unscathed, but seeing his father and brother both murdered and hearing the dying screams of his mother so frightened him that he also began to scream. The Indians pursued and lanced him and left him for dead.

Mr. Mason heard the boy's screams and started with gun in hand to meet the boy. While still in sight of his house, he tried to shoot at the Indians but his gun failed to fire. Mrs. Mason then, with her two year old child in her arms, ran to meet him with a box of caps for his gun. Before she could reach him, the Indians had killed him, and then came on and killed her and her child. While at Cameron's house, the Indians captured a little girl eight or nine years old. She was tied on behind one of the Indians and, of course, watched all that was done. They pillaged both houses, but left a girl of six years in one house and the baby with the dead body of its mother in the cow lot. For some unknown reason, these two were left unhurt and uncaptured.

The Indians then made their exit but soon after encountered some Californians, who discovered that the Indians had with them the little white girl. The Californians then went in pursuit, and were rapidly gaining on her captors when the little girl was loosened and fell to the ground unhurt. The Californians returned with the child. A day or two elapsed before this awful murder was known, for the Indians had gone some distance before the little girl was discovered and rescued and returned to her home. In the meantime, a man who lived several miles from the scene, in passing, discovered that the Camerons had been killed. On going into the house, he found the six year old girl crying piteously and also heard the little one in the lot crying next to the body of its mother. The baby held up its little arms, as if begging for help, which was given to both children as soon as possible. Then the bodies of these poor, unfortunate parents and of their children were buried with all the care and in the best manner that the condition of the country would permit.

The little boy who was lanced and left for dead, having revived, walked about six miles in the direction of Jacksboro. Leaning against a tree in a sitting posture, he was found dead. After the little girl was returned by the Californians, she told the people that there was a white man with the Indians who had killed her father. This lead to the arrest of some men by the name of Willis, of very bad reputation. There were three or four of them—brothers—who were all arraigned before the vigilance committee. Why it was that this committee, after a thorough investigation of the case and after having such convincing evidence from such an innocent source, failed to execute the villains was never explained.

The Willis men, having learned that Mr. Cameron had a large sum of money in his possession, went with these Indians to kill and rob the family. The little girl said, when asked about the killing and the events of the massacre, that a man with red whiskers and long red hair was with the Indians. This man, she said, broke her father's trunk open. When the man under the most suspicion, Bill Willis, was brought before her, she at once said, "This is the man who broke the trunk and took Pa's money and killed Ma." Even in light of this plain evidence, they were turned loose. Some three or four years later, they stole a number of horses and carried them to Mexico. While returning through western Texas, they were again arraigned before a vigilance committee, and three of them were lynched. Thus ended the career of one, at least, of the assassins of the Camerons and the Masons.

FATHER TACKETT'S INDIAN FIGHT

Father Tackett, as he was generally known, was a Methodist preacher. While he was a very devout man and one who had, by his earnestness and devotion to Christianity, won the universal confidence and esteem of the frontier people, he was also a man of great courage.

Not far from the time that the effort was being made to place the Indians upon reservations established in Young County, and the government was trying a pacifying mode of treatment toward them by furnishing them with food, clothing and schools, and doing what it could to civilize them, Father Tackett settled in a rather rugged country. He established his home not far from the two reservations on the Brazos River, twelve or fifteen miles apart. He lived on Fish Creek, about equidistant from each of these. My brother-in-law, Judge Z. E. Coombes of Dallas, then a young man, was employed to teach the Indian school at the lower agency. He was intimately acquainted with Father Tackett and said of him, "He was a very worthy man, active in his Christian ministry and a very bright Mason. He was ever on the side of right, and ready to stand to his convictions."

Early in the year 1859, the Indians were, notwithstanding the kind of treatment they were at the time receiving from the government, giving great trouble to the settlers as they had always done—perhaps now just a little worse than before. At this time, Father Tackett saw one of his cows, that had just left the herd which was out on the range, come in and keep walking about shaking her head. Upon investigating the cause, he discovered an arrow stuck in her neck. This, of course, told the story. He knew from experience that the Indians were at mischief. So, taking his three grown sons—Jim, George and Lyke—each armed with a shotgun and six-shooter, they took the back trail of the wounded cow, which they could follow without difficulty since there was snow on the ground.

They followed the trail some two miles to the foot of a mountain, which was ever after this called Tackett's Mountain. Here they found the herd, but were cautious not to go into the rough breaks, where the Indians could take the advantage and waylay them. They rounded up their little herd and started for home. The Indians were watching them from the top of the mountain, and at once they went in a roundabout way and got in a gulch where the cattle were sure to cross in going home. When the cattle reached where the trail crossed the gulch, they were startled by something and Lycurgus, thinking that it was an animal of some kind, presented and cocked his gun. At this, the Indians arose and Lyke shot the only one who had a gun.

This opened the fight and the Tacketts, with deadly aim, emptied their guns into the eleven Indians. The Indians, evidently thinking that the guns were all that they had to shoot with, and that they were now unloaded, dropped their bows and arrows. Drawing their scalping knives, they made a rush toward the Tacketts. As they did this, the Tacketts opened fire with their sixshooters. The Indians wheeled and ran like scared turkeys, leaving four of their number dead upon the ground and several others wounded badly. The old man and one of his sons were slightly wounded, being only glanced by arrows and not seriously hurt. The Tacketts were not inclined to be bloodthirsty people, and did not follow up the advantage thus secured, but turned immediately for home with their cattle.

The old gentleman, in talking with Colonel Sams who now resides here at the town of Benjamin, said, "Like Paul, speaking after the manner of men, I have seen the elephant one time but I don't want to see him anymore." Not long after this, the old man and most of his family moved back to Parker County and lived not far from Spring Town where, several years after this, I met him at his house. His sons, at least some of them, remained with the cattle on the ranch and still kept them there even through the dark days that followed the Civil War. One son (not mentioned above) named Chas. or A. C. Tackett, remained until buffalo hunting was engaged in for a livelihood by so many frontiersmen. He then followed the buffalo, hunting until they were driven far out upon the frontier and killed off.

Here I want to express an idea that may give some information that does not seem general among the people. It is often said by people who were not present during the time of our Indian troubles, that when those immense herds of buffaloes were being so ruthlessly slaughtered, that it was a great pity that those valuable animals were killed in the manner they were. But this I conceive to be a grand mistake.

The killing of the buffalo removed the main source of food supply from those roving bands of hostile Indians and caused them to depend upon some other means of subsistence. In this way, the peace policy has been made a success and this could never have been done while the buffalo remained, as is now shown to be a fact by the way in which the government has to issue rations to them on their reservations. They have now learned to look to this source for food and clothing supplies, and have in consequence thereof become more friendly toward the people and the government. They are now being taught something of a domestic life and are becoming more of an agricultural people, laying aside their barbarous ideas, and seeking better things. Some of them have homes and many of the comforts of life around them.

It is true that this trend toward civilization is a slow process, but the trend is in that direction, and the Indian is now forced to learn lessons that they would never have learned in any other way. And the white man sees that it is easier and cheaper to feed them than to fight them. This is the only principle on which the giving of homes and other advantages, to a people who did not seem to want them, can be justified. "If thine enemy hunger, feed him; if he thirst, give him drink." Anyone, even now, going among the old warriors of the Comanches, Kiowas and Apaches, and seeing that dark scowl upon their faces, will be forced to think of the dreadful murders that they have committed and in which they found such great delight, and in which they would still take so much pleasure had they the power. But now they are shorn of their power, and those evil passions are controlled. This should be a great blessing to them, as it is to those people who have found so many happy homes in this frontier country.

Although it did seem merciless and cruel to a great many good and wise people of a former day that the buffalo should be killed in the manner they were—their hides taken to the market and their valuable carcasses of meat left as food for the coyote—we, who live to take a retrospective view of the past can see in almost every event the hand of an All-Wise Providence, who controls the destinies of nations and individuals. The buffalo were killed just in time to permit the recuperation of the range for the use of those immense herds of cattle which were soon to take their places and supply food that was capable of being handled to much more advantage, and transported to the markets of the north and the east. It was so much needed there for the upbuilding of a race of people far superior to the master of the buffalo and antelope, and one which was destined, too, to rule the world in the interest of human liberty and happiness.

I had myself some experience in raising cattle on a range over which those herds of buffalo drifted, on my ranch on the Little Wichita River in Archer County. There, they drifted over and through the range, and I learned by that experience that they would have been very destructive to the cattle business of the west. Again, we can now see the effective influence of the long-range guns that were used by the buffalo hunter, not only in removing from the range that great destroyer of grass and vegetation, but also in the protection of the people from the savage master of the buffalo.

After the buffalo, soon came the cowboy with his Winchester and sixshooter, supported by indomitable courage, who completed the preparation that for years had been progressing unchecked, for the habitation of the once Great American Desert. We who live today in that once borderland—where, once was the war whoop of savages, the groans of his wounded victims who lay scalped and dying, the screams of his captives, and the sadness and sorrow of those homes bereft of father, mother or loved ones—can, with pride in the superiority of our own race, view the immense strides that have, in so short a time, been made toward the betterment of the world at large by the annihilation of the inferior people. Today we find that quietude, happiness and contentment have replaced sorrow, sadness and fear, and that Christianity fills society with pleasure; life is sweet and is worth the living. The change is worth all it has cost; a thousand times its cost. The old shaggy buffalo is all gone, but let him go! We may now, awake or asleep, rest in our quiet homes without the fear that the murderous savages will break in upon our peace or slumbers with their hideous yells. May the wheels of progress continue to roll onward and upward and away from those dark and gloomy days of the past, until even the memory thereof shall fade from our lives and cease to have its depressing effects.

Capture and Escape of Mrs. Shegog

Since I began to write a history of our Indian troubles, Mr. and Mrs. Gray have several times mentioned the capture of Mrs. Shegog as one of the most horrifying incidents that they have ever known among all the tragic events that have occurred in Texas. Colonel Sams, who also lives here at the town of Benjamin, was very familiar with this incident and speaks of it in the same manner. Not long after it occurred, I moved up on Black Creek, not far from where it happened and just on the trail which the Indians followed when they committed this cruel deed.

The killing and scalping of people was no new thing in that part of the country, for during the War and for years thereafter, this section of the country was accustomed to frequent visits from the Indians. The people were in continual dread. The Indians came skulking in through the Upper Cross Timbers and therein concealed themselves until they were ready to make their sweep over the country. Prior to the time of which we are writing, the Indians had faced no trouble in killing on the Upper Red and Pease Rivers all the buffalo that were necessary for a sufficient supply of meat to last them through a long raid into the settlements. As such, large numbers could raid together, which was the case in this instance.

Mr. Menasco came into the country as a young man from Arkansas, and lived for some time in Navarro County where he was married to Judge Brown's daughter. Afterwards, he moved into the northwest part of Denton County and settled on the head of Clear Creek. When the War began, he had been there long enough to have become very well and comfortably fixed in his home. In the early part of the War, his father came to live with him. Although the Indians had been into the country on a number of very destructive raids, they had never molested his home. Mr. Menasco and his father, nevertheless, were in continual suspense, waiting and hoping for the time to come when the government would give them safe protection.

Captain Shegog, who married a sister of Mr. Menasco, lived within a mile and a half of him. One day in the winter of 1868, when Captain Shegog and Menasco were out on the range hunting stock, a large band of Indians numbering about three hundred, came down through the cross timbers. Evidently, they were Comanches from high up on the Red River and, on account of their large numbers, they were moving along intrepidly in daylight and camping at night, as if they were in their own country among friends. This whole body of fearful savages moved through the country, leaving devastation and death as they went. They carried on their brutal work, as if they had no thought or fear of being restrained in their destruction.

On this sad and fatal day, the two oldest children of Menasco were at the home of Captain Shegog. Their Menasco grandfather learned that the Indians were in the country and went over to Shegog's to bring the children and their aunt, Mrs. Shegog over to the Menasco home where they could be in a safe place. But about halfway to reaching their destination, they were suddenly surrounded by a large number of Indians. The old man was cruelly murdered and Mrs. Shegog, with her child a year or more of age, and the two little Menasco girls who were four and six years of age, were taken as prisoners. The Indians then went to the Menasco house and, surrounding it, began whooping and yelling like infuriated demons.

Of course the Indians intended to kill, rob and carry off as captives the inmates of the house, as might suit their monetary fancy, but Mrs. Menasco, taking her stand by the door with her gun presented, told them that some of them would die should they attempt to enter. Just think of this brave woman, standing there undaunted in the presence of such dreadful danger, seeing her sister-in-law and her own dear children there, captives at the hands of merciless savages! Calmly and determinedly, she stood for home and for fireside. Those cruel old warriors read in her appearance the fate of one who dared enter there. So they turned to the horse lot, took two valuable horses and departed.

This large band of Comanches went far down into the settlements, evidently intending to sweep the vast herds of stock horses off of the prairie country, but in this they failed to a great extent. They went down below the town of Gainesville and then, turning back west again, they camped for the night only a mile or two from the town. They had not taken their prisoners far before they killed Mrs. Shegog's child, but took its mother on with them. One night, when a cold norther was blowing and snow was falling, she slipped off into the darkness and escaped to the hospitable home of Sam Doss where, almost frozen, she was kindly cared for and returned to her home. No doubt that, on account of the extremely cold weather, the Indians failed to conduct a search for her.

Early the next morning, they moved on, but before they had gone many miles on their way, they left both of the Menasco girls, who were perhaps already frozen to death at the time that they were left. The body of one was found one month later, but that of the other was not found until nearly three months had passed. The Indians found that the horses on the prairie were too thin of flesh to bear rapid driving, so they took but few of them away. The cold hindered them on their return and it was said that many horses perished in the snow storm. Not long after these heartrending scenes, both families moved down to Pilot Point where they lived and prospered.

Murder of the Huff Family

It was nearly ten years after the close of the Civil War before the government forced the Indians into submission. As stated previously, this was not so much on account of the sectional feelings engendered by the war as it was from the mistaken policy of the government in the management of the Indians. In fact, the Indians were themselves mistaken as to the motives of the government in the adoption of this pacifist policy. They evidently thought that it was evidence of weakness in white people, resulting from the Civil War, and not until they were taught some pretty severe lessons did they learn any better. General Mackenzie, with a good, strong force, followed them to their home at the foot of the plains. He found them in a deep, rugged canyon—a tributary of Tula Canyon—and, making a sudden attack upon them, captured their horses and left them afoot. Then, driving the horses off to one side, Mackenzie had the animals killed. This so impressed the savages that they made an unconditional surrender.

Just before this surrender occurred the last raid that was ever made into Wise County. It was conducted by about thirty or forty Comanches. The trial and conviction of the noted chiefs, Satanta and Big Tree, by the civil authorities of Texas, had given assurance to the people. They began to move out into the new country and find homes for themselves there. The raiding band of Comanches had crept down through the new settlements pretty much in the same way that they had done for so long, except that they showed greater trepidation and more caution. After they got as far as Denton Creek, they started a drive on the horses of the country.

This raid was made in August of 1874. Under the bright moonlight, they passed up the divide between Catlett and Black creeks, within a mile and a half of my house, driving a large herd of horses. The tramping of hooves and the neighing of horses could be plainly heard at my house. They had so many horses that it required their entire force to keep the animals together. The night was far spent before they passed through my neighborhood. They reached the edge of the Upper Cross Timbers at sunrise.

They were soon passing through the new settlements that were forming on Briar Creek, a tributary of Big Sandy Creek, where Mr. Huff, the subject of this sketch, was living. Here there were several families who lived within about a half mile of each other. Near Mr. Huff's house was another house that had been completed, but Huff's was built of logs and did not have the cracks chinked and as such was not safe against the attacks of Indians. So when Mr. Huff heard the Indians coming, he ran over to his neighbor's house with the intention of getting a gun with which to protect his family. But by the time he reached his neighbor's place, the horses which the Indians were driving were passing on each side of his house. When the Indians behind the horses reached Huff's house, they could see plainly through the cracks of the house Mrs. Huff and her two grown daughters. Gathering around the house, the Indians shot Mrs. Huff. The daughters, springing out of the door, were both shot down while their father looked on, powerless to render them any assistance.

All of the men in the neighborhood went in pursuit of the Indians, and were almost in hearing distance of them when the Huff women were killed. Pushing on, the men overtook the savages about two or three miles from Huff's house, just as they were entering a heavily timbered bottom. The Indians abandoned the horses and split off into small groups which, of course, could not then be trailed. The men rounded up the horses and returned them to their owners. But these poor unfortunate women were the last to have their blood spilled as victims of the cruel savages in Wise County, and the poor father and husband was completely heartbroken. It was thought for a long time that Mr. Huff would lose his mind from the effects of the murder. I met him frequently for several years afterwards and he seemed the saddest man I ever saw. He thought of how near at hand was the relief that was coming and knew that if his wife and daughters could have lived but a few short months longer, how comfortably fixed they would all be in their new home. These thoughts intensified the poor old man's sadness.

KILLING OF KEENON'S AND PASCHAL'S FAMILIES

This account was given by a small boy—the son of Mrs. Keenon—who made his escape on that fatal night. This account was included in the Texas Ranger, A. J. Sowell's, history. Of course, the Rangers went directly to the place of the murder and learned all that they could, but since the only survivors were a little boy and a little girl, the only eyewitness accounts came from them. The report, as given by Mr. Sowell, located the place on the line of Wise and Montague, but it actually occurred in Montague County, not far from Victoria or Queen's Peak. Here, we will give verbatim quotation from Sowell:

"While in camp on Big Sandy, news was brought us of the killing of several women and children on a small creek, thirty miles north of us, on the line of Wise and Montague Counties. We lost no time in getting off with eighteen men, well mounted and armed, to the scene of the slaughter, and by rapid riding arrived at the place before night, which was at Keenon's ranch. But we soon discovered that it would be impossible for us to follow the trail, as it had snowed since the Indians were there. As we rode up, we saw seven new-made graves on the north side of the cabin under the trees. The settlers from down the country had buried the dead.

"There were only two ranches west of this—Colonel Bean's and O. T. Brown's. Bean was absent at the time. His ranch was two miles west of Keenon's. The Keenon house consisted of only one room, about twelve by fourteen feet, made of logs. There was a small field south of the cabin. At the foot of the hill near the creek, on the northwest side, about two hundred yards from the house was a small lake. There was a crib of corn. Keenon himself was not at home when the Indians made the attack on his ranch and massacred the helpless inmates.

"We dismounted, walked to the door and looked in. It was a horrible sight. The door was torn from its hinges and lay in the yard, covered with blood. Blood on the doorsteps, blood everywhere, met our sight. The inside of the cabin was like a butcher's pen. Quilts and pillows were scattered over the floor, covered with blood. The dress which Mrs. Keenon wore was hanging across the girder which extended from one wall to the other. It had been hung there by some of the party which buried the victims. The dead were as follows: Mrs. Keenon and two of her children, the widow Paschal who lived with the Keenons, and three of her children.

"We obtained the particulars of the attack from one of the Keenon children, a boy of eight years old, who made his escape on the fearful night. He said it was about ten o'clock at night; the ground was covered with snow and it was very cold. The inmates had all gone to bed, except Mrs. Keenon who was sitting by the fire, smoking. On the north side of the cabin was a small window with a shutter that fastened on the inside with a wooden peg entering a hole in one of the logs. The door was on the south side. Everything was quiet and still on that cold winter night. The children were all asleep, and probably dreaming sweet dreams which seldom visit the couch except in innocent childhood. Suddenly, with a crash, came the end of a rail through the frail shutter, bursting it wide open. The hideous painted face of an Indian looked in, and he began to crawl through the window and into the cabin. One brave man or woman armed with an ax or hatched could have held them at bay, but poor Mrs. Keenon was timid. She sank to her knees and began to pray and beg for her life.

"As fast as one Indian got through, another followed him until nine hideous wretches stood inside. By the time the balance of the inmates of the house were aroused, the children began screaming and the work of death commenced. Pen cannot describe the scene. The cold and lonely night, far out in the western wilds; the painted faces of the Indians lit up by the wood fire; the frantic and heartrending cries of women and children; the sickening blows of the tomahawk etc. make one shudder to think of it. Who can blame a Texas Ranger for putting his sixshooter to the head of a wounded savage and pulling the trigger, as they often do in battle when they are the victors?

"It was during the confusion that the little boy made his escape through the very window by which the Indians had entered. He received a severe cut with a knife in the hip as he went through, but succeeded in making his escape from the house and hid himself until the Indians left. Crouched in some bushes near the corn crib, he watched and listened until all was still. The work was done and the fiends had reveled in the blood. This boy displayed a presence of mind that was truly astonishing for one of his tender years. Before he escaped from the house, he noticed the number of Indians that had entered and when they came out to take their departure, he counted them to see if they were all leaving. The Indians had left their horses at the lake and had come to the house on foot and, as the ground was covered with snow, the boy could plainly see each form standing out in bold relief against a white background. He left his place of concealment and watched them until they mounted their horses and disappeared over the snow-clad hills toward the west.

"Being satisfied that they would not return, he came back to the house and entered. What a sight for a boy of his age to behold! His mother lay near the hearth, with three arrows in her breast, tomahawked and scalped. Some of the children were killed in the bed, while others lay on the floor in pools of blood. One of his sisters was crouched in the corner with her throat cut, and there was at least a quart of blood in that corner when we arrived there. The widow Paschal was lying on the door shutter in the yard and had three broken arrows in her breast which she had broken off in an attempt to pull them out. She was scalped, as well. The youngest child, about eighteen months old, had been caught by the legs and its head dashed against the wall of the house. It was then thrown through the window onto the frozen ground.

"The boy brought the youngest child, his little sister, into the house and laid her before the fire, where she recovered. While in the house attending to his sister, he heard a noise in the yard and, on going to the door, he was Mrs. Paschal sitting up on the door shutter upon which she had been lying. She looked horrible—covered with blood and her scalp taken off—but the brave boy went to her. She asked him for a drink of water and, as there was none in the house, he took a gourd to the lake and brought her the water. Mrs. Paschal drank the water and immediately expired.

"On looking around while we were there, I saw the old lady's pipe lying on the hearth where she had dropped it, about half smoked out. We also saw a bent arrow spike in one of the logs just above the bed. It had been shot at some of the children on the bed, but missed its mark. The shaft had been removed. The next evening after the massacre, a settler passed the house and was hailed by the boy who told his tale of woe. The man took a hasty view of the victims, then galloped off to give the alarm. The next day, the dead were buried and the news carried to the Ranger camp. We we arrived, the ranch was deserted and the children carried off and cared for until the arrival of their father, who was away somewhere with another of his children. This no doubt saved his life.

"As we could accomplish nothing in the way of following a trail that was covered with a fresh fall of snow, after an hour's stay, we mounted and started for camp, vowing vengeance should we ever meet the red man face to face. Some time after our first visit to the Keenon place, a small group of us returned for a load of corn. Mr. Keenon had returned and was preparing to move away from the frontier. Our captain, hearing of his intended departure, purchased his crop of about three hundred bushels. I was detailed on this trip as one of the guards and saw the little girl who was thrown out of the window and so nearly killed. She was very lively and when we asked her where the Indians had hit her, she tucked her head down so that we could see the back of it. It still looked quite discolored and bruised. The boy's wound had not healed yet and he looked pale and thin.

"I want to say for this little boy, that I never knew one of his age to display greater genuine courage, nor more thoughtfulness. Wounded as he was, when he returned to the scene of blood and carnage, his first thought was, of course, his mother. But finding her there scalped, covered in her own blood and lying still in death, his next thought was of the little one—the smallest and most dependent. When he had looked all around among the poor murdered victims and failed to find her there, he began searching for her. No doubt she had been his daily care, and day by day he sought to amuse and please his little sister of one and a half years. Not finding her on the inside of the house, he went out around that lonely cabin and, having found her where she had been thrown by those cruel fiends in human form, he tenderly lifted her from the cold bed of snow and brought her in to their poor, lifeless mother. Before the warm fire she soon revived and what a source of joy it must have been to his bleeding heart to find signs of life in even one of those he loved.

"While he was caring so kindly for the dear little one, his ears were attentive to every sound. It was a moment of the most intense interest as he caught the feeble murmurings of his dying aunt, Mrs. Paschal, out in the yard. In trying to retrieve water for his dying aunt, he bravely hurried to the lake where he had last seen those dusky foes who had just wounded him and killed his loved ones. But he went undauntedly to that dangerous spot and brought water for his poor, suffering aunt. I want to say again that I never saw any greater courage or thoughtfulness. The long weary night and nearly another day have passed before his watchful eye catches sight of the first person to pass near, when the poor little wounded soldier staggered to the door and hailed for relief.

"Brave and gallant generals lead their armies to victory and often to death, and their friends at once seek to have their deeds of valor placed of record, that they may not be forgotten. Cool, undaunted courage is worthy of admiration. Patriots who are willing to stand at the post of duty in time of great danger should be kindly remembered and a biographical sketch of this little boy ought to be written, as it were, in letters of gold, and should embellish the pages of every Texas history book. Since I have been writing this book, I have felt mortified, in reading other books and gathering data from every reliable source, to find that all the suffering, privation and hardships have been borne by our early settlers, as they pushed forward, opening the way to civilization and standing as faithful sentinels between the wild savage foes of civilization and the peaceful home of the older settled sections of the country, without there ever having been an effort made to honor their noble deeds.

"Is not this civilization a blessing? Have they not blessed the land in which we live and consecrated it with their blood? Could this country ever have been rescued to civilization without someone having to go to the front and bear the burdens and the suffering, just as our frontier people have done? Shall all their deeds of valor be forgotten, and shall they be misjudged and placed among the selfish and adventurous, seeking only their own welfare? I do hope not! I see there has been talk of having a meeting of the old settlers for the purpose of forming a regulation association to hold annual reunions in memory of the suffering and sacrifices that they have made.

"Some people, who do not properly understand this question of frontier life and frontier defense, seem to look upon the adventurers, who pushed their way into the wild and perilous West in order to get homes in the new country, as trespassers on the rights of the roaming bands of savages that have been, from time immemorial, fighting and killing each other when not engaged in murdering and plundering the white settlers. But if it was wrong for us to move out and occupy this great land, that is now the home of the happy millions; if the principle advocated by these mistaken, sentimental people were carried out, this vast domain would still be left to the warring savages and the wild beasts of the forest; the crowded millions would look in vain from the shores of the Old Country across to this beautiful land. The few scattered inhabitants would still be living just like the beast of prey, except that they were more destructive to each other than the beast.

"The vast forest, the fertile soil, the navigable streams and all these wonderful blessings that the God of nature gives would be lying unused, while thousands of His creatures would be suffering and perhaps perishing for want of them. But God has decreed that men should live by the sweat of their brows, and now under His well-directed providence, we see the sons of toil transforming the wilderness into fruitful fields and blooming gardens, and dotting it over with beautiful cities. Our navigable streams are filled with steaming vessels carrying our bounteous products to our seaports, to be turned into the commerce of the world, that others may be blessed by our labors. Our internal improvements have gone on and on, until now our whole land is checkered over with railroads, whose long rolling trains are, in connection with our great ocean steamships, taking our produce to almost every land where it serves to bless and sustain the hungry millions.

"We have always extended the hand of welcome to the homeless of the earth, inviting them to come and share with us this great land of peace and plenty. Can we, then, be called trespassers? Is not the earth the Lord's, and the fullness thereof? Should not all of God's creatures share alike the blessings that flow from His bountiful hand? This is God's country, and we are his creatures. The Indians, too, are His creatures, and are entitled to their portion of His blessings. Are we giving them their portion? Do they stand equal with the whites in the blessings of the land and under the laws of the country? No! Not only are they equal; they are the favored few. They are not only given the very best of homes in the land that they have chosen, but they are fed and clothed by the white people, and the best of schools and school buildings are furnished without any cost to them, and all the blessings of civilization are offered them for the taking. The descendants of those whom they have cruelly murdered and scalped have brought these great blessings as a gift, in return for their cruel, merciless treatment. The great principle that Christ taught the world is being carried out: 'If thine enemy hunger, feed him; if he thirst, give him drink.'"

Yankee Who Wanted to Kill an Indian

While talking with Uncle Dan Shipman, as he is gener-ally known, I heard a brief account of some of the Indian troubles that occurred in Erath and some adjoining coun-ties, along about the beginning of the Civil War. I will now mention one of the facts given in the beginning of his ac-count, which is in keeping with what has often happened in other places. I do this in order to do simple justice to all parties mentioned. I do not think it will at all excuse the desperate cruelty and fiendishness which they exhibited all through these long, dark years of terror and trouble.

A man who had come from down East kept saying that he wanted to kill an Indian before he went back. He was told by the people that the Indians were very friendly in this neighborhood; that the Indians would visit their homes and bring them wild meats, and that they were as kind as could be; but that, if they were mistreated, they would never forget it, and were sure to seek revenge. Nonethe-less, the man kept saying that he must kill one before he left, as it might be his last chance.

Sure enough, one day he got a chance and killed a young Indian whom he caught alone. This so enraged the Indians that they moved way back into the mountains on the west and were soon on the warpath and seeking revenge. Quite a band of them came in quite unexpectedly and killed an old man named Johnson. After stealing quite a number of the best horses in the country, they started back toward the mountains with their booty. On the way, they hap-pened upon two young ladies going to church and, taking them captive, stripped them of their clothing. When passing Stephenville, which was then still a small town, for some reason the Indians turned the girls loose. To use Uncle Dan's language, "They got sorry for them." But I think this was a mistake. They must have been influenced in some other way, for their actions afterwards showed that they were strangers to pity and that real sympathy never touched one of their hearts. The girls crept into town after wandering about for a long time, were kindly cared for and at once returned to their homes.

Uncle Dan Shipman also told me of another raid which occurred not long after the one just described, which no doubt was the result of the same cause. This time they had a larger force and penetrated further into the settlements to the edge of Johnson County. The Indians captured two children, whom they were taking back as prisoners. But when they had returned as far as Erath County, two large bodies of scouts had been assembled—one from Duffau and one from Paluxy. The scouts found their trail and succeeded in attacking them on both sides.

The children, seeing that the Indians were closely pressed, took advantage of the situation and made their escape by jumping from their horses and hiding behind some large rocks. The white men at first took them for Indians, and one man fired at them. The children immediately cried out, "Don't shoot! We are white children!" Then the man who fired the shot, who was so startled at the thought of shooting a white child, rushed immediately to them. His doing so probably prevented their recapture by the Indians.

The Indians were driven from the battlefield, and the little folks were secured, as well as a large number of horses and mules that the Indians had stolen from the settlers. The children were carried safely back to their parents by the scouts who had made the successful fight, and the horses and mules were returned to their owners. The red rascals were so hard pressed that they had to scatter like partridges in order to save themselves. The parents, it is unnecessary to state, were overjoyed at the return of their children. Uncle Dan tells of an amusing circumstance which occurred while the scout was being put together to intercept the Indians:

"It was Sunday morning, and a runner was sent to the schoolhouse where the people were assembled for preaching. The preacher, who saw the young man come in and speak to the captain of the minutemen and then to the man who had sixshooters on, although having just taken his text and begun to preach, stopped and asked what was the matter. The runner was answered that the Indians were in, and that all men were wanted. The preacher answered, 'Well take them, and as I have taken my text, I will preach to the women.' So he took his text, and the women all took the fright and left the poor preacher, who took his text home with him. The men went on the scout and succeeded in killing several Indians, without the loss of a man."

Riggs Killed, Little Girls Escaped

As we have, at the close of the account of the killing of the Keenon and Paschal families, written a eulogy of the Keenon boy who, I think, was really worthy of more praise than I was capable of giving him in such a short space, I will now relate as near a parallel for it as I have ever read or heard in my life. While the killing of Riggs and his wife occurred at a much earlier date than that of the Keenons and Paschals, it is equally touching and pathetic.

The killing of Riggs and his wife occurred near the central part of the state, probably in Bell County, now one of the most populous and wealthy counties in Texas. At the time of this occurrence, just prior to the Civil War, the settlement of that part of the state had just begun. The Indians had been of little trouble for a long time, so the people apparently felt secure in their homes. They were not careful to carry their arms, as is usually the practice in frontier countries, and they were caught off guard. Mr. Riggs lived in the valley of Noland's Creek, not far from the cedar brakes. A man named Pierce and a boy named Elms lived with him.

On a very bright, beautiful morning in the spring of 1859, a band of Indians came into that neighborhood and were stealing horses, plundering houses and doing everything they could to terrorize the settlers. While the Riggs family were rejoicing over the beautiful spring and quietly enjoying their peaceful home, the bloodthirsty savages unexpectedly came. They first came upon Mr. Pierce, some distance from the house, and killed and scalped him. They then came across Mr. Riggs and the Elms boy. They had just started with a wagon and team to go to the cedar brakes after timber. The Indians at once surrounded them and, catching the boy, they began to whip him, when Mr. Riggs made a run for the house. They then turned the boy loose and ran after Mr. Riggs. The boy escaped and hid himself so securely that the Indians never found him again.

Mr. Riggs was successful in reaching the house and barred the door securely. When the Indians discovered that the house was secured, they moved off a piece from it. Riggs then, with his family and children, started to the house of a neighbor. When the Indians saw them leave the house, they rushed upon the family. They killed and scalped both the father and mother, but left the baby, just old enough to begin crawling, by its mother in a pool of her blood. The Indians took the two little girls, ages six and ten, away with them. This is when the most interesting part of this awful tragedy began. The following was written in a letter to the author, Wilbarger, from Bandera County on April 25, 1886:

"After murdering and scalping my poor father and mother and leaving little brother crawling about in the blood, the Indians placed sister and myself up behind them on their horses and carried us back to the house, which they plundered. They carried the beds out of the house and emptied the feathers from the ticks, and wrapped them around themselves and began dancing and making sport with them. They then started out with us behind them on horseback. They came upon a bunch of horses under a tree and, rounding them up, they snared one of them, and then pushed on until noon. When they stopped to eat dinner, they separated into two squads, keeping sister in one and myself in the other. I went to where my sister was but they would not let me stay. After they had feasted upon the victuals which they had taken from our house, they started on again without giving us anything to eat. They would change me from one horse to another occasionally, and on we traveled until the middle of the afternoon.

"They came upon a man, whom they chased on horseback until they caught him and then, shooting him with arrows, they killed him. I can remember seeing him bathed in blood and hearing his piteous groans. But they did not tarry long with him and, went on for some distance, until they came in sight of some cow hunters. This surprised and excited them, and caused them to ride very fast. When the Indians were changing me from one horse to the other,

I fell, which, together with the fast ride, hurt me so that I was unable to walk after. Sister, seeing that I was hurt, jumped off from behind the Indian that carried her. He held on to her dress until he passed near a stump, which she caught hold of and freed herself from the savage grasp. After she recovered sufficiently, she came to where I was. She, being about four years older than I, carried me all she could, and then I walked all I could as we started back in the way we had come.

"About dark we reached an old house where no one was living and we remained there all night. It was very cold and sister pulled off her dress and, wrapping me in it, nursed me all night. Next morning, we started and followed a road which led to a house, which we soon reached, but the people were all away, forted up from the Indians. However, we went into the yard and stayed awhile until a man came riding up. We were at first frightened and went around the house to hide from him. When he came to the house, he hallooed, and we went to see him and found that he was a white man. Then we related to him what had happened to us. He then placed us upon the horse and took us to the next house, which was Captain Damon's. We stayed there until our friends came after us."

The above, no doubt, is authentic and well deserves a place in every book that is being written to inform succeeding generations of what terrible cost of blood and suffering our now peaceful and happy land was purchased from the possession of those savage Indians. It is not a mere fit of sentiment, but of simple justice, that those who pushed to the front and were the victims of these excruciating trials should, at least, be gratefully remembered, and that their descendants should be repaid in some substantial way. I wish I had the words at my command to properly eulogize that noble little Rhoda Riggs who, at such a sacrifice to self in that lonely deserted cabin, took the clothing from her own body in order to keep her sister warm. At the age of only ten years, to show such maternal care, is truly wonderful.

The Indians, after all their cruelty and merciless treatment, safely escaped. They were probably the last to enter Bell County. They carried away a number of horses and several scalps of innocent white people, although they were followed some distance by two different companies, who at last gave up the chase and let them go.

Outrages in Uvalde County

I have at this time many friends who lived in this northwestern portion of the country in those perilous frontier times who are giving me the benefit of their experiences and are writing them down for me. Of course, they rely principally upon their memories, but such incidents as we wish to relate here are of such a nature as to make a lasting impression upon the memory of anyone who has experienced them. We hope, in the main, that their stories are perfectly reliable.

A few days ago when I was visited by Judge A. C. Tackett, I asked him if he remembered certain events. He said, "Of course I do, just as well as if it had occurred yesterday." In consulting Mr. James Rigger, another man from Wise County who was present in those fearful days of Indian warfare, I found him to be even more familiar with the events which had occurred in that county than was I. In giving the account of the outrages in Uvalde and adjoining counties, I shall follow largely a personal account given by Mr. Kennedy in Wilbarger's history:

"A man named John M. Davenport was killed on the Sabinal River. He had at one time been the captain of the minutemen there and was a fearless man, ever ready for duty. He left a wife and several children to mourn his loss. On the day after he was killed, the citizens gathered together some fifteen men and, joined by Lieutenant Hazen of the U. S. Army with about the same number of men, they took the trail of the Indians, and followed them. They overtook them on the second day and at once charged upon them. The Indians soon retreated, but would occasionally stop and make a stand, only to be forced to move on as soon as the white men would make an attack. Thus the running fight kept up for nine miles, when the Indians plunged over a very high and nearly perpendicular bluff, where the white men stopped and abandoned the chase.

"Three Indians were killed on the way, and several more were wounded. Davenport's scalp, gun and hat were recovered from the Indians. Three of the citizens and Lieutenant Hazen were wounded. The citizens were loud in their praises of Lieutenant Hazen and his men for their gallant conduct in this fight. These Indians were Kickapoos and Lipans from Mexico, and they evidently got a setback here that went a long way toward holding them in check afterwards."

Mr. Kennedy also gives an account of the Indians killing an old man named Schroon, who had been a member of Castro's Colony and was following the frontier on westward. He was caught unarmed and was killed without making any defense. The same party killed a Mexican boy about eighteen years old, whom they shot through the heart. Of this, Kennedy says, "He was dead before I came to his assistance, not five minutes afterward."

The Indians did not have the time to scalp their victim. This young Mexican was working for Kennedy and his body was removed to Kennedy's house. Kennedy says, "We always kept dried beef and bread and shod horses ready for such emergencies. So in a short time we were off after the Indians, leaving the dead Mexican boy in the house with my wife, who told us not to turn back until we had settled accounts with the Indians. About two hours after we started, we were joined by General W. B. Knox with two men. They were under the impression that some mules which had been stolen from their wagon were in the possession of these Indians.

"Towards night, we lost the trail on the west side of the Sabinal, about six miles above the main wagon road. Near this place, we found the bodies of two white men—Mr. Huffman and Mr. Wolf. The bodies were lying about twenty feet apart and the throat of Wolf was cut from ear to ear. Not far off, we also found the dead body of an Indian, whom we supposed had been killed by Wolf. The Indians had placed the body near a live oak tree with his blankets rolled around him, and his bow, arrows, shield and other equipments placed near him, according to their custom.

"We supposed, from the signs on the ground, that Wolf and Huffman had made an attack upon them. I knew

Huffman personally. He was a bold, daring fellow and, on several occasions, when riding the express for the U. S. government, had been known to attack bunches of Indians alone.

"After leaving this point, we finally found the trail again, going up Blanco Creek to about twenty-five miles above the crossing. The trailer, W. A. Crane, who was riding in front, suddenly halted and, looking back, pointed to the Indians' saddle horses grazing in a small glade about fifty yards distant on the right of the creek. I immediately motioned to the men to dismount, and myself dismounted. We had the horses securely tied and detailed two men to guard them. We intended then, under cover of a small ravine, to get in between the Indians and the cedar brakes and thus cut off their retreat. General Knox was opposed to this movement, and thought it best to make a direct charge on them.

"Contrary to my judgment, Knox's approach was carried out. The Indians' horses stampeded upon our approach, giving the Indians timely notice of our presence. They secreted themselves in the dense cedar brakes near their camp before we could get a shot at them. However, we captured everything they had—bows, arrows, guns, shields, horses and camp equipage. They had just barbecued a fat yearling, which was very acceptable to us. Before daylight, we were back at Sabinal with the stolen caballada of horses. The next day, we went up and buried the bodies of Wolf and Huffman in one grave."

"Hog-My-Cats" Bowles

A man by the name of John Bowles, and generally known as Hog-My-Cats, lived on the Leona River, and upon one certain night during the full moon he had a corral of very fine horses shut up near his house. A band of Indians, discovering the horses, had crawled up and, having opened the gate gently, had just succeeded in driving the horses out of the lot when the dogs began a fearful barking. This ruckus aroused Bowles. He and his sons ran out with their guns, drove the horses back into the corral and drove the Indians away.

Hog-My-Cats was not satisfied simply with getting his horses back. He wanted to teach the Indians a lesson. So, taking his large double-barrel shotgun and loading it with blue whistlers, he ran around to where he knew the Indians were sure to cross the river and secreted himself there awaiting their arrival. It was not long before the Indians came up and halted right over where Bowles was hiding. Bowles took deliberate aim with his old blunderbuss and fired. Two Indians and one horse came rolling over the bluff, dead as hammers by the time they reached the bottom. A third Indian was badly wounded and was trailed for several miles by his blood. Bowles' sons, hearing the roar of the gun in the night air, at once went to their father's assistance. When they reached the top of the bluff, they saw him standing on the body of a dead Indian, exclaiming, "Well hog my cats if they steal any more of my horses!"

Poor Bowles was, about a year after this, in the woods looking for one of his horses that was out with a bell on. The Indians had gotten hold of the bell and it is supposed that they decoyed him into a thicket by ringing it. They killed Bowles there, but his body was not found for several days, in spite of the citizens' thorough search which lasted nearly a week. When he was found by his son, Green, his body had been partly devoured by wolves.

The Whipping of Henry Shane

Henry Shane, a young man about eighteen years of age, was employed by Major Riordan to attend his stock on Pinto Creek, ten miles west of Fort Clark. While out on the range, a party of sixteen Indians charged upon him, took him prisoner, whipped him severely with a rawhide strap and tied him on the back of a mule. They went off in a northwesterly direction, traveling until two or three o'clock in the morning, when they halted and camped. They took young Shane from the mule and, after amusing themselves by whipping him again severely with rawhide straps, put him to bed with an old Indian that smelled worse, Shane said, than a turkey buzzard.

The next morning, they tied him on the mule again and started off. About nine o'clock in the morning, they stopped for the purpose of getting some breakfast and un-tied young Shane. Just then, it so happened that a party of U. S. soldiers, guided by a Mexican named Rookey, discovered the Indians and at once made a charge upon them. Shane, taking advantage of the confusion that ensued, fled for his life and liberty. In doing so, he received an arrow through his arm, compliments of one of the Indians.

Shane said that he heard a great deal of shooting after he fled, but did not know who was being whipped, the Indians or the U. S. soldiers. He did know one thing...that he had been pretty badly whipped himself! He wandered about for four days with nothing to eat but a piece of dried beef, but eventually made his way back to Riordan's ranch, pretty badly worsted by his trip with the Indians. Major Riordan was very glad to see him again and bought him a fine new sixshooter, which he subsequently used to square accounts with the Indians, on several different occasions, for the whipping they gave him.

MRS. ROBINSON DEFENDS HER CHILDREN

A. M. Robinson and Henry Adams were killed at Chalk Bluff on the Nueces River about March 1861, while on their way to Camp Wood. A. M. Robinson had been on the frontier for many years. He was a stockman and farmer, and was sometimes employed at Fort Inge to trail and fight Indians. He was married and left a wife and nine children, all living in Uvalde County, except one daughter. There were sixteen Indians in the party that killed these men. From the signs, it was evident that they two men had stopped to make coffee, and the Indians had crept up behind some driftwood and killed them before they had time to use their guns. After killing them, the Indians went to Robinson's house, about seven miles from Chalk Bluff, and attacked the inmates.

Mrs. Robinson was on a visit to one of her neighbors at the time and, hearing some noise, went to the door and saw the Indians chasing her children. A boy of sixteen, named George, who had a gun, fired upon the Indians and was immediately shot down himself. The balance of the children ran towards their mother, who soon joined them, and in her desperation she endeavored to drive the Indians back by throwing rocks at them. But such weapons were of no avail against guns and bows and arrows.

They shot a girl named Kirby, about fourteen years of age, who was visiting the Robinson family but, strange to say, made no attempt to shoot Mrs. Robinson and the other children. They all escaped safely. Savages esteem courage more highly than anything else, and probably the Indians refrained from killing Mrs. Robinson and the rest on account of her heroic efforts to defend the children.

Although Miss Kirby was shot with arrows, lanced, scalped and left for dead, she recovered and eventually went to California. The Indians plundered Mrs. Robinson's house, taking everything that they fancied. Cutting the beds open, they scattered the feathers about the place and appropriated all the provisions they could carry off. One of

their acts in particular was very strange indeed. After killing Robinson, they pulled off one of his socks. Finding his
portrait in the house later, they took it from the wall and
placed it on the floor. They then placed the sock they had
taken from his foot across the picture.

Mrs. Kincheloe Badly Wounded

In October 1866, a party of Indians came to the house of Robert Kincheloe, opened the front gate and rushed into the yard. There was no man at the house at the time and Mrs. Kincheloe, Mrs. Bolin and Mrs. Kincheloe's child were alone there. As soon as Mrs. Kincheloe discovered the invaders, she seized a Spencer rifle and made an effort to shoot them. Since she didn't understand the gun well, it failed to fire. One of the savages said to her, "No bueno," which was intended to mean "No Good." The two frightened women then shut the door and pushed the table against it, and both jumped upon the table.

The house was made of pickets and, in places, there were spaces through which the Indians could shoot their arrows. They shot Mrs. Kincheloe a number of times, from which wounds she soon grew so weak that she fell to the floor. Before falling, she gave the gun to Mrs. Bolin. No sooner had Mrs. Bolin taken the gun than one of the Indians shot her through the heart and she fell forward, dead upon the floor.

As there was now no one to guard the door, the savages forced their way into the house. But before they did, Mrs. Kincheloe, although so badly wounded, crawled under the bed and hid herself. When they came in, they turned everything over in search of plunder. One of them discovered Mrs. Kincheloe and lanced her several times. The poor woman fainted from pain and loss of blood, and the Indians, assuming she was certainly dead, left her and went in search of more plunder.

The little boy, when the savages came in at the front door, ran out of the house through the back door and, slipping into the brush, hid himself until the Indians were gone. When they were out of sight beyond the mountain, he ran to a neighbor's house about three miles away where he gave an account of the awful fate of Mrs. Bolin and his mother. A man named Oburant at once aroused the neighborhood, and they went in pursuit of the Indians. The party soon lost the trail and returned home.

Mrs. Bolin's seventeen year old daughter was not at the house when the Indians arrived but, seeing them approach, climbed into a thick bunch of cedar and was thus securely hidden from them. She noticed that the Indians came and went in the direction of the place where a Mexican was herding Mr. Kincheloe's sheep. This circumstance, connected with the further fact that the Indians knew where to find Mr. Kincheloe's money in the house and the fact that they knew no men were at home at the time, led to the belief that the Mexican was connected in some way with the Indians in the killing. When the guilty scoundrel was arrested, he attempted to escape and was killed. Mrs. Kincheloe, though so badly wounded, finally recovered and many years afterward was living in Sabinal with her children.

JUDGE MARTIN & HIS SERVANT KILLED

Some time before the Mexican War, there was a man named Gabriel Martin who lived on the Red River and was a close personal friend of General W. E. Dodge. He was in the habit of going out into the upper river country to hunt, always taking a negro man with him who was a good hunter and a fine shot. One day, he took his little son with him on a buffalo hunt. After they had been on the range for several days, they were attacked by a number of Pawnee Indians, who suddenly surprised and overpowered them. Judge Martin and the servant were killed and horribly butchered, and the son was taken captive.

When the sad news was by some means conveyed to the settlements, Judge Martin's brother-in-law, Mr. Wright, got two or three men to go with him and went in search of the little boy. Fortunately, they met with General Dodge, who was then on his way to the Pawnee village in order to make a treaty with them. After several days' travel, they reached the Pawnee camp where, after their peaceful mission was properly explained, they were kindly received. The head chief, who was a rather old man, made quite an eloquent speech in his reply to General Dodge. Of course, the communication was carried on through an interpreter, and they all seemed pleased at the recognition given them by the white men. I wish that I had the ability to tell about this conference as well as General Dodge told it to me when I met him, several years after the incident, in Fort Worth.

General Dodge, some of the officers of his regiment and a company of soldiers were present at the council. After explaining in a very kind way the object of their visit, General Dodge told the Indians that they must be accountable to his government for the murder of Judge Martin and his servant, and the capture of his boy. He told them that the Comanches had said they had the little boy with them and that they must surrender the boy. But the Pawnees denied knowing anything of the murdered man or his son. The demand was urged very strongly upon them, yet they continued to deny it until a negro man who was living with them and spoke clear English came to the council and told them such a boy had recently been brought to their camp, and that they had him now as a prisoner. This appeared to greatly excite the whole council and there appeared to be a strong feeling among them, especially among their chiefs.

As those who have met him know, General Dodge was a man whose bravery and determination could well be depended upon. He at once told the old chief that the council would stop right there until the boy could be brought in. In order to give them further assurance of his peaceful intentions he told them that, before starting out to visit them, he had bought two little Pawnee girls and a Comanche girl who had been stolen from them several years before and that the Osages, their enemies, had held them for a high ransom. He stated that he had the girls with them, and would not give them up unless the boy was produced. He also demanded the surrender of a Ranger, named Abbe, whom they had captured. They acknowledged the capture of the Ranger, but said that the Comanches had taken him and put him to death.

After a long consultation, the Pawnees were assured of the truth of the white men's claim of having the little girls when the General had them brought in. They at last sent out and had the little boy brought in. He was almost naked or, at least, was lacking clothing in the same manner as the Indian children. When the boy reached the council, unaware of what was going on, as he passed among the white men, he said, "What are these white men doing here?" In response to this, General Dodge asked his name, to which he promptly replied that it was Matthew Martin. He was then embraced by General Dodge and tears rolled down Dodge's cheeks.

The three little Indian girls were then brought in and were at once recognized by their friends and relatives, who were wild with joy at receiving them safe. The old chief was so overcome that he cordially embraced General Dodge and each of the officers and, with the strongest expressions of gratitude at this evidence of the white man's friendship, the tears streamed from his eyes.

Now, this council, which at first seemed to stand in doubt, was one of the most cordial and friendly, and the old chief had Dodge and his men well supplied with food. They remained a day or two, and a friendly treaty was consummated with the Pawnees and closely observed by them for a number of years. The little boy was safely conducted back to his home and his overjoyed friends. Before we close this account, we must say that the rescue of this sprightly boy was due largely to the firmness and undaunted courage of General Dodge.

Capture of the Ball Boys

Two families lived in Wise County named Ball. Jim lived on the head of Black Creek and his older brother, Moses, lived further down the creek about three or four miles. Each brother had a son, nine or ten years of age. There was a passway for the Indians near each of their homes. They could go in at one pass and out at the other.

One day both families were at the house of Jim Ball, and they sent the two boys to the spring for water. When they failed to return from the spring after a time, their mothers feared they had been captured by the Indians and went looking for them. The path to the spring lead through thick brush and undergrowth, and the boys could not be seen after they were a short distance from the house. As the mothers went down the path toward the spring, they saw the buckets which the boys had taken with them sitting by the path, but the boys were not to be seen.

When they reached the place where the buckets were, they saw the fresh tracks of horses crossing the path. By the buckets, they saw moccasin tracks which at once told plainly that the dreaded red man had their little boys. These were two very affectionate mothers, and Mrs. Jim Ball's grief was especially heartrending as she looked for the footprints in the dust. She traced them very plainly to where they met the moccasin tracks but could not find them any further. There, they knelt and kissed the little tracks the children had made before they were taken by the Indians.

Not far from the same time, but I think on a different raid, they took Bill Freeman's boy who was about the same age of the Ball boys. I do not remember the particulars of his capture, but they were taken by the same tribe and all three were held for about three years, when by the untiring energies of Carlo Ball, son of Moses Ball, they were found. He, with Mr. Freeman, purchased the boys from the Indians by paying a lot of saddle horses for them. Bob Freeman and Moses Ball's son had become so infatuated with the wild life of the Comanches that they wanted to go back to them, and it was with some difficulty that they were restrained from doing so. Several years after they returned, I was living near Moses Ball. His son would come and visit us, and talk of the Indians in a way that clearly indicated his fondness for their manner of living.

Captain Earheart Kills a Red-Headed Indian

After the close of the Civil War, when the men had been at home long enough to replenish their supply of horses. They were taking better care of their cattle, which had advanced in price and were bringing considerable money into the country. People could buy the necessary horses and arms. The citizens of the frontier began to take more interest in their property, and sought to protect both life and property more solicitously than they had ever done before. With their experience on the frontier and knowledge of the habits of the Indians, they were well prepared to take care of themselves.

The country had been so stripped of horses during the War that they were considered valuable, and the settlers tried hard to keep those which they were able to obtain secreted away in some secluded place where the Indians would not be liable to find them. Commonly the horses were placed in a small prairie surrounded by timber, where they could not be seen for any great distance and were lariated or hoppled so that they could graze in security. If the Indians were known to be in on a raid, the horses were guarded during the night.

In about 1870, Captain Earheart was at his ranch during the full moon and, learning that the Indians were in on a raid, he, with some of his hands and perhaps some of the neighbors, went out to the back of his farm and staked several good horses on the fine grass. The men were secreted in the fence corner to watch the horses, with one man remaining on guard while the others slept. Toward the end of the night, the guard noticed the horses were looking off down the fence as if they saw something unusual. He at once woke the others and told them what he had noticed.

Captain Earheart, being an old frontiersman and understanding all the Indian maneuvers, began watching closely in the direction in which the horses were looking and he soon discovered an Indian who was slipping along the fence toward them. The Indian would crawl to the corner and then dodge quickly around it, then crawl to the next corner in the same way. Captain Earheart told the boys to wait a little. Taking close aim with his gun upon the fence corner, when the object appeared at the corner the next time, he fired, and the Indian rolled into full view.

Several Indians off in a different direction from the one who was killed now showed themselves, but finding that the white men were on the alert, they withdrew. They had evidently discovered the men watching the horses. The Indian who was killed had been assigned the job of crawling on to the guard and killing him, so that the others could steal the horses. Daylight soon came and they went to the Indian whom Earheart had shot. To their great surprise, they found that he had red hair and blue eyes, but was otherwise to all appearances an Indian. No doubt he had been stolen when he was a child and was raised by the Indians to be just as cruel and bloodthirsty as they were.

No one cannot help but think of what had probably transpired at the time of his capture; of the murdered parents or, perhaps, of their broken, bleeding hearts, of their years of watching and waiting in suspense for his return, of their untiring efforts to find some clue as to his whereabouts; of the many pangs suffered by that poor mother over the loss of her darling boy whom she never ceased for one moment to think of. Better far that she might carry to her grave that lovely image of innocence left upon her memory, than that she could realize to what a depth of depravity he had at last been lead by his merciless captors.

Captain Stephens and His Men Surrounded

In 1872, companies of minutemen were organized along the frontier for the better protection of the people from the attacks of Indians. The men who returned from the army, bringing with them old army guns and ammunition, added greatly to the safety of their homes. Many had managed to get improved guns and ammunition, so the country was at any time prepared to give the Indians a pretty strong fight. In Wise County, George Stephens was captain of the minute company and had with him the very best of Indian fighters. Among them were Tom and Henry Jennings, John Hogg (brother of Governor J. S. Hogg), Vincent and Archie Watson, and many others—tried, true brave men.

In 1873, a large band of Indians made a raid down through Montague and Cooke Counties and, on their way back through Wise County, Captain Stephens with twelve or fifteen of his men, pursued them and overtook them near Buffalo Springs. The Indians numbered about one hundred, well armed, and out in an open country about seven miles northwest of Buffalo Springs on the head of the east fork of the Little Wichita River.

Captain Stephens, not intimidated by their larger numbers, opened the fight by charging them. The Indians shot several of the Rangers' horses at the first round and, fortunately for Stephens, there was a deep brushy branch just behind where they could take shelter. Falling back into it, they were immediately surrounded by Indians. The Rangers shot with such deadly aim that they succeeded in keeping the Indians back. The Indians killed and captured all their horses and took everything they had except their guns. Captain Stephens was wounded in the upper part of one of his hips, which rendered him unable to stand alone, but he was able to crawl upon his hands and knees.

When it became dark and the Indians had withdrawn for a short distance to eat their supper, the white men crawled upon their hands and knees down the narrow, deep channel of the branch. They succeeded in passing beyond the

Indian lines without being discovered. It was then about thirty miles to the nearest settlement. Captain Stephens had to be supported by a man on each side of him with his arms extended over their shoulders. Traveling in this manner, they finally reached Mr. Martlett's on the head of Big Sandy Creek, where they secured a wagon and team.

John Hogg and the Jennings boys were very stout men, and as brave and true as were ever known anywhere. Not only this, but they were close friends of the gallant George Stephens. One of them on each side of him, as it were, carried him out of what would have been certain death, for the Indians no doubt kept the siege through the night, thinking that the next morning they could easily kill or capture the whole bunch of white men. John Hogg told me afterwards that he wore nearly all the skin off his feet. He, like his brother J. S. Hogg, is a very large man and rather inclined to be fleshy. And since the weather was warm, the men must have been nearly exhausted when they reached Martlett's. But once they secured transportation, they were home in a short time and ready for another scout.

The Last Indian Raid in Jack & Wise Counties

About the 8th or 9th day of July, 1874, over four hundred Indians came down the Brazos River and passed through Young and Parker Counties. This band went around on the prairie north of Fort Worth and went back through Wise and Jack Counties. This was after the Rangers had been put into service by the state, and Lieutenant Boyd with about sixty Rangers followed the Indians until they reached Lost Valley, in the western part of Jack County. Here, the Rangers stopped, their horses almost worn out by travel. The Indians were largely in the majority and their horses were fresh. Some of their horses had been recently stolen and were in fine condition.

Lieutenant Boyd held a council with his men to discuss these circumstances and to determine whether or not to attack or to first go into camp and get a mount of fresh horses and reinforcements. They decided by ballot, and the vote stood six majority for going back to camp and getting reinforcements. Upon reaching camp, Captain George Stephens remarked that he could have whipped all the redskins that could be gotten together. This comment reflected on Captain Boyd's bravery, and Boyd told Stephens he intended to take men and go make an attack. Stephens said no, that he would take forty men and go whip the Indians himself.

Lieutenant Boyd very kindly and patiently warned Captain Stephens that the Indians were well armed and well mounted, and in very strong numbers. Nevertheless, it was only a few minutes until Stephens was off for the scene of battle. Boyd had wisely left sufficient men to watch the Indians' movements and keep up appearances, in order to hold them in check. When Stephens left camp, one of his neighbor's boys, Will Glass, wanted to go with him, but was told he had better not go. Glass was determined, however, and at last was permitted.

When Stephens and his men reached the place where the Indians had been, there were none to be seen. The men who had been left to watch their movements assured him that they were nearby in ambush, as they had been watched very carefully and were not seen leaving the locality. Captain Stephens was confident that he would succeed and made very little delay in ordering a charge upon the place where they Indians were last seen—in a rough canyon in the brakes. No sooner had they reached the small valley in the canyon than the Indians began to pour in upon them from every side.

The Rangers were forced to retreat down the canyon to Cameron's Creek, carrying with them the bodies of young Bailey and Will Glass, who had both been killed in the first round fired by the Indians. Several other men were wounded and sixteen horses were killed, which left many men afoot. The brave Captain Stephens made all the resistance possible against such odds, and thus prevented the redskins from scalping his killed and wounded men.

While they were retreating, Blue Roberts became separated from the command. Unable to reach his comrades in their distress, he made his way to Fort Richardson, twelve miles distant, where he secured a force of U.S. troops and returned as quickly as possible. Captain Stephens and his men were still retreating and fighting as they went, with but little hope of escape, when the troops came in sight and the Indians retreated. Owing to their superior numbers, they were allowed to move quietly away without further pursuit.

A strange thing occurred in connection with this raid: Will Glass, before starting out, said that he was sure he was going to be killed, yet when his best friends (among whom was Captain George Stephens) tried to prevent his going, he seemed the more determined, so they gave way and permitted him to go. Sure enough, he was killed in the first volley fired by the Indians.

Strange as it may seem, in every instance that I have known, where a man had a premonition of this kind, it has always proven true. Will Glass was not only a great favorite with the Rangers, but his death caused very deep grief in the community where he lived. His parents were almost prostrated with sorrow, and the question could be heard on every hand, "Why didn't they prevent him from going after they knew of the premonition?" But thus it is in many instances of this kind, almost like predestination. This is one of those things in life which surpasses our understanding, and perhaps is best for it to remain for solution in the future state, where the secrets of every heart will be revealed.

Just one year after this raid, perhaps some of the same Indians made another raid through the same country. They did not go so far east as before, but went back through Wise and Jack Counties, killing the Huff family in Wise County and stealing horses all the way until they reached the same locality where they had defeated Captain Stephens the year before. On this raid, there were but a few Indians. They were overtaken by Lieutenant Ira Long, from near Decatur, with about 40 Rangers near the same ground where Captain Stephens had been defeated. In the charge made by Long, nearly all the Indians were killed, without the loss of a single white man, and only a few horses.

As Lieutenant Long led the charge, one of the Indians turned upon him. Long shot him from his horse. At the same instant, the Indian shot the Lieutenant's horse, and both men fell together. By this time, nearly all the Indians had been shot down. The one who fell so near Lieutenant Long was believed to be dead, but was in the act of aiming a Winchester at Long when he was killed by a bullet from one of the Rangers' rifles. It was discovered that, instead of being an Indian, he was a blue-eyed white man with fair skin. He was sunburnt, half naked and in regular Indian garb.

About this time, an old Indian squaw, seeing that her death was inevitable, turned toward the Rangers and raised her blanket from her breast, to reveal that she was a squaw. She had been fighting as hard as any of the Indians, so the boys shot her down just as they had done the others. One thing that made the men less inclined to show a squaw any mercy was the fact that squaws were more cruel and merciless to captives than even the bucks were. It was thought that often, when prisoners were put to death, that many would have been spared had it not been for the cruelty of the old squaws. However, this was not without excuse on the part of the squaws, for in many instances the squaws had their own sons or close friends killed by the white men. As such, they were more revengeful.

It was never known, as far as I can learn, whether the white man who was killed in this battle was one who had been taken in childhood and raised as an Indian or whether he, like many others, was a renegade. He may well have been a fugitive from justice from the United States or elsewhere, who could no longer live in civilized society. On this account, many a man took to making his home with the savage Indians and became even more savage than they.

Right after this fight, I moved my cattle in upon a range near Lost Valley where this fight occurred. My cowboys were often out upon the battleground and found many bones, bows, arrows and other relics of this, the last battle ever fought with a band of hostile Indians on our frontier.

OLIVER LOVING KILLED ON THE PECOS

Oliver was the father of J. C., George B. and Joseph Loving. When the Northwest Texas Cattle Raising Association was organized in 1876, James C. Loving was chosen as secretary, and he continued to fill that position until his death in 1902. During the greater part of this time, he made his home at his ranch in Lost Valley in Jack County. No stockman in the state was better or more favorably known than he. George B. Loving for many years operated extensively in buying, selling and shipping cattle but finally established the Texas Live Stock Journal and was its editor until not long before his death. Joseph Loving is a very respectable citizen of Parker County, living near Mineral Wells.

Oliver Loving came with is family from Louisville, Kentucky, in 1867 and, settling in Weatherford, was engaged in moving cattle from Texas to Colorado and Wyoming. On one of these trips, having passed across the plains, they came to the Pecos River. Since the herd had been without water for some time, the men were afraid to let them into the valley until they could learn whether they were liable to strike an alkali lake. Mr. Loving, accompanied by a one-armed man named Wilson, went on ahead of the cattle in order to learn about the water. When they arrived at the Pecos, they were surprised by quite a large band of Indians charging upon them.

The first shots that were fired broke Mr. Loving's right arm and so disabled him that he knew that he would be unable to successfully resist the Indians in battle. Finding that escape by flight was next to impossible, he plunged into the water and concealed himself under some overhanging brush where he remained for several hours. Fearing discovery by the Indians should he come out of the water on the same side where they were, he swam over to the west side of the river.

Striking the road that lead up the river to Fort Sumner, he started in that direction. Being chilled from having lain in the water so long, the warmth caused by the exercise of walking was very pleasant. Having lost so much blood from his wound, he was greatly weakened and he lay down in the shade of a small bush to rest. There, he fell asleep and during his nap, screw-worms entered his wounded arm.

Finally he was awakened by the noise of a train of Mexican wagons on their way to Fort Sumner. They received him in their train and conveyed him to Fort Sumner as early as they could, where he received all the care and attention that could be furnished at that post. However, in a short time he died from blood poisoning. He was a very strong, vigorous man and, had it not been for the 125 mile journey up the Pecos before he received medical attention, he would no doubt have survived.

Loving's sons, as well as his whole family, were active, energetic people and the Lovings of today are among the leading citizens of the country. Although their father lost his life handling cattle, his children were nearly all engaged in the cattle business. The Lovings' ranch was in a beautiful valley near the western part of Parker County which is still known today as Loving's Valley. Mr. Wilson, who was with him at the time he was wounded, was mounted on a very fleet horse and made his escape from the Indians. He is now a very prosperous stockman.

THE THRILLING HISTORY OF THE FRIENDS

In the early settlements, perhaps about 1867 or 1868, in the dark days after the Civil War when the country was in an unprotected condition and the Comanches and Kiowas were making frequent raids, there lived a family by the name of Friend in Bosque County. These have always been known as the Reconstruction days when troops were placed in our country to watch the people to keep them in a state of subjugation more so than for their protection. The Friend family consisted of father, mother, grandmother and four or five children. They were all accustomed to that continual watching in which all frontier families are so well trained.

The certainty of very eminent danger to which the people were continuously exposed so impressed everyone that it became a part of their very nature to always be on watch. I speak from experience on this subject, for I passed through this terrible ordeal myself and had a family around me that I very dearly loved. The anxiety for their safety was resting upon my heart daily and was often the subject of our conversation. In this way, the children as well as the older ones were kept ever on the alert and watching for the dreaded Indians.

The Friends, although living in a remote part of the country, were probably about as secure as other people. At least this was the case when they were at their home, one of the dearest and most sacred spots on earth to every family. At that home was their every earthly interest—the roof which sheltered them from the storm, the hearth around which they gathered each night as one by one they came in from the busy labors of the day. Oh, how thankful they were when each one was securely sheltered in their home.

One day, some members of the family saw quite a large force of men on horseback approaching their home and, after watching them for awhile, concluded it was a group of stockmen and cowboys since such men tended to travel in a strong force to protect themselves from the Indians.

After the Friends concluded it was only a bunch of stock-men, they felt perfectly at ease and were thrown entirely off their guard and were wholly unconscious of the dreadful fate that awaited them.

Suddenly, Indians came pouring in on their defenseless home. They seized George Friend, seven years old, his sister who was nine years old and his brother who was twelve years. These children were at once securely tied and the balance of the family put to death right before their eyes—even the old grandmother. The father and mother were killed and scalped. The little captives were then untied and placed on Indian ponies. The Indians took the children, as well as anything else in the house that suited their fancy, off to the mountains with them.

In plundering the home, the Indians destroyed everything of value that they could not carry away. Every little cherished momento, everything that made the home so lovely, was obliterated and the work of hardening their captives' hearts to that cruel, heartless life to which they are doomed. Little George was forced to carry his own mother's scalp, no doubt, to harden him and destroy those tender ties of love implanted in his bosom by those kind parents that had been murdered before his eyes.

Before entering in on the history of the Friend children as captives in the hands of those merciless wretches, we will say that this account was given by George Friend to Mr. and Mrs. James Cadey of Hefner in Knox County, Texas. They gave it to me as they heard it related by him and both seemed to think that it was perfectly reliable. Many of the old settlers today will often mention the incident but they, of course, can't give a detailed account as George Friend gives it.

In his statement, he says that there were other families in their neighborhood that were killed at the same time. He only gives the name of the Davis family that lived quite near the Friends and did not give a detailed account of their murders, but we can judge from what he says that this band of Indians had been on an extensive raid. At the time they charged on the home of the Friends, they were on their way back to the mountains and were evidently from different tribes, as the oldest boy was separated from George and his little sister. They never saw him afterwards.

The second night after they were captured and being taken back into the mountains, the Indians thought the children too tired to attempt an escape and left them completely unconfined. But late at night, while the Indians were all in deep sleep, George and his little sister made their escape. They managed to elude their pursuers all the next day and went up into a mountain where they found a small cave filled with the drifting leaves of surrounding trees. Fatigued and weakened by hunger, they crept in among the leaves and slept soundly until late the next morning when the Indians discovered their hiding place.

The children were again made captives and, although for some time they were kept where they could see each other they were no allowed to talk to each other at all. They were kept as slaves or property of certain Indians and, while the other Indians would take some interest in the children in trying to teach them Indian language and customs, they were regarded as property of their owners and could be traded off at any time.

Finally, old Sitting Bull bought George for the sum of one pony and some tobacco, and began to train him to be like the Indian boys. He taught him to love to ride horses and hunt with bows and arrows, all of which George took to very readily. In fact, I knew a number of boys in those days who were brought back from captivity but wanted to return to the Indians. The excitement of the chase and the wild life seemed to have a charm for them that they couldn't give up very well. Once a boy had formed a fondness for these things, he was ready to accept all of the habits and customs of the Indians. In fact, George Friend says that not only did he love the Indians and their wild ways, he actually came to hate the white people and looked upon them as his bitter enemies.

George says that after he was traded to Sitting Bull, before he was to be taken away from his sister, they were allowed to talk to each other. They got together out beside a little tree and kept up a busy talk for as long as they were allowed. When they were forced to part, they mingled kisses with their tears and their parting was a bitter one. It must have seemed very strange to those hard-hearted wretches who had torn them from their homes and loved ones.

George says that as they were traveling along a valley one day, they looked up against the mountain and saw smoke coming out of the chimney of a little cabin. They at once made a rush for this little house and killed the man and his wife who were living there. Then the old chief took up the bright, beautiful baby girl that was lying on the bed and, tossing her up in the air, he placed his bowie knife under her as she came down. The blade pierced her body through and through.

After a terrible shudder, she was dead and the old brute pitched her over on the bed. Looking at the scene for a moment, he walked off, trembling like a leaf and took his seat. When the other Indians noticed him, they asked what was the matter and the chief, patting himself over the heart said, "I hurt right there." Pointing to the little dead baby, he shook his head as if a touch of regret had come to him. But is it possible that one who had always delighted in bloodshed and murder, of killing parents and kidnapping their children, that the killing of an innocent infant could stir a single thought of remorse or regret?

In this instance, there is only enough regret expressed to indicate that they are a sort of human being, but that they are cultivating the very worst there is in human nature. In fact, they try to surpass each other in doing the worst things that they are capable of doing, and those that can take the lead in this become leaders among them. George says at one time, while he was on a raid with the Indians stealing horses and doing all the devilment they could, he happened upon a fellow holding a horse by a rope that was drawn through a window. George slipped up and cut the rope, and ran off with the horse. This was such a clever feat that, although he was only a boy, it gave him great prominence among the Indians.

After he had been among the Indians for 9 or 10 years (at which point he'd have been sixteen or seventeen,) while on a raid upon the white settlements, George was among the band of Indians surrounded by General Miles and his men. Each and every member of that band was killed or captured, and George Friend was among the captives. When General Miles was looking them over, he pointed out to his men that there was a white boy among the Indian captives. Looking under his breechcloth, they could plainly see that he was a white boy and, of course, they at once set out to find out who he was.

When it was made known to George that he was recognized as a white boy and that the men sought to learn his name and who he was, he at once determined to make his escape back to the Indians. As he had been allowed to retain the pony on which he was captured, he has said that he told General Miles he was running away and mounted his pony. He made a break, whipping his horse at every jump and refusing to heed demands for him to stop. General Miles cut down on him with a long range gun and killed the pony upon which George was riding.

When the pony fell, the fall broke George's leg and, of course, stopped him from any further escape efforts. He was taken to a government hospital in Indian Territory where the kind treatment he received made quite an impression on him. During the long period of time that he was cared for there in such a kind and pleasant way, he learned again to speak our language. He seemed to return to himself to an extent, recalling some early scenes of his captivity, of the murder of his family, of having to carry his mother's scalp and of escaping with his sister. It was a complete and thorough change to him in which his life was being fully reversed. Because of the use of the word "Friend" so often repeated to him, his name too came back to him. In this way his identity was fully established.

As the story was given to me, there was a U. S. Senator who learned about the boy and set out to find out George's history. When he had gotten it pretty well, he told George Friend all about it. Although George had been refusing to wear anything other than his Indian garb and still seemed so determined to return to Indian life and habits, when he was made to understand how they had killed his people and treated him and his sister so badly, he became an almost inveterate hater of the Indians.

It is said that one day he was passing by where some Indians were playing cards and got into a conversation with them. They insisted on his taking a hand with them and, as he had his gun on him, he got off his horse and opened fire on the Indians. He killed three out of the five right there in a pile while the others made their escape by flight.

Having his leg broken when his horse was killed from under him was a turning point in George Friend's life. Although it made a permanent cripple of him, it was the very best thing for him, as it kept him in restraint until he fully understood all about his family being so cruelly murdered. By the kind treatment of the white people, he was enabled to contrast the cruel vicious lives of the Indians with the peaceful lives of white people.

By some means, the Missionary Baptist people got hold of George and educated him for the ministry. They did an excellent part by him but he had become so thoroughly aroused in regard to his captured brother and sister, he was determined to find them. For this purpose, he made lectures over a great deal of Texas and followed each with inquiries about his people. While in New Mexico, George says that at one place where he made a public talk, a man came to him and asked where he would make his next talk. When he answered the man, the fellow said that his wife would be there to hear George even if she had to kill a horse to get there. Sure enough, she was there at the next talk. When he was telling of his and his sister's experience in trying to escape and of being recaptured, the woman didn't hold back any longer.

She walked right up to where he was speaking and asked him to let her see his scar the scar on his chest. Opening his clothing, he revealed the scar and the woman then began to scream out that George was her long lost brother. Suffice it to say, there was quite a scene enacted right there and who could blame them? After having endured such trials as each of them had, by some unseen power or at least by circumstances that nobody can account for, they were thrown together again.

Although she had lost an arm and he was a cripple in one leg, it became the aim of both of them to find the other brother from whom they were separated at the time of their capture. This will be very difficult and almost a miracle for them to happen upon their brother as they happened upon one another. It is very commendable, though, for them to show such an interest in their brother, as it shows that they appreciate the wonderful change that has come over their lives. It may seem wrong that George, after receiving the benefits of education, has not gone on to fulfill his calling as a Baptist minister. But this he meets with the proposition that he esteems it as his imperative duty to try to find his brother. When we consider that George was a captive himself, experiencing the vicious customs of the Indians, and that he knows that there is a better life for everyone that will avail themselves of it, it is perfectly natural that he should want his brother to be aware of such a life.

It is possible that there are many white men living the Indian life who are wholly unconscious of there being anything better. This has been demonstrated by the fact that once in awhile there has been a white man killed that was among the Indians and engaged in warfare against the white people. The red-headed Indian killed by Captain Earheart while trying to kill the captain in Wise County was perhaps one. The blue-eyed man killed in the last fight in Lost Valley in Jack County by Sentry Ira Long is another. These were both men in something like middle age and had long been with the Indians, sporting long hair and regular Indian garb.

The case of George Friend is a rather strong argument in favor of the idea that there is something civilized in the blood that runs in a white man's veins, for as soon as George was brought in contact with a better life and a better influence, he at once made the change in his way of living and his way of thinking. But on the other hand, many of the full-blooded Indians that have been educated were certainly in good society while they were being educated, but when they returned to their own people they at once took up the old blanket life and sunk to the same social level in which they were raised. I could call some of these by name, but will refrain from doing so, as a number of them are now embracing the Christian religion. We will only hope for the betterment of them in the future.

No one can be entirely independent of his surroundings nor can anyone scarcely rise above his environment without some assistance from others. Perhaps there are many of the young Indians that, if they had proper surroundings, might make very good people. At least there are good reasons why we ought to make an effort to lift them up to the higher and better life. Our greatest regret in closing this story of the Friends is that we cannot give a detailed account of George's sister while in captivity. In these closing lines, I would like to state for George, should this book come to your notice, that I would be glad to have the account of your sister's life and your sanction for what I have here written in this book about yours.

Why I Never Fought the Indians

One reason that I never did fight the Indians was that it always seemed to me like I could make a better race than I could a fight, so I took chances on making the run. While living in Wise County, in the early 1870s, I would go in the wintertime and kill buffalo meat enough to do my family until the next summer. It was certainly the finest meat in the world. In the winter following 1874, I went with my brother-in-law, Edward Brannin, and a man by the name of Pool, to kill a load of meat. We took a wagon and a good pair of horses, a good saddle horse and plenty of feed to keep our team in good strong condition. I rode an extra good running horse. The object in having this horse along was to use him in getting the buffalo, but at the same time he would be useful in case of a flight. We went out west of the Upper Cross Timbers, on the head of the west fork of the Trinity and on the Little Wichita in what is now Archer County. The buffalo were very plentiful and we soon secured a fine wagonload of meat.

By the time we were ready to start home, it was getting nearly to the full moon. As every frontiersman well knows, that was the time for the Indians to make raids in order to steal horses. On the evening before we were to start out, I told my companions that I wanted to kill a buffalo calf and get his robe for the children to tumble on on the floor at home.

We found a herd of 300 or more buffalo grazing quietly in a valley. I had my saddle horse in good trim and, taking my buffalo gun, started into the valley to select a nice calf. When the buffalo started out of the valley, they headed directly for our camp, which was three miles away, and I put in after a very fine fat calf that ran alongside his mother. As I could outrun them, I got up close to them in the herd. They sprang out of the herd but continued in their course pretty much in the direction of our camp. After running them for a mile or two, I felt that I was running old brown Jim too far and knew that I might need him for another kind of race, so I ran close on to the calf and shot him. When my companions arrived, we took off the fine glossy robe from the calf and also took his fat hindquarters. We hung them in an old mesquite tree nearby and started into camp.

After we had gone a half mile or so, we found the tracks of about twenty ponies. We followed them for two or three hundred yards, discussing whether it might be a bunch of Indians or a bunch of cowboys. We had about concluded that they were Indians, as the ponies were all without shoes and were all small like Indian ponies tend to be. Just then we came to where they had broken into a run and had spilled a lot of dried buffalo meat. The meat was prepared in the way that we knew Indians arrange their meat for a raid, so we didn't follow the tracks any longer. Instead, we made straight for our camp.

We knew very well that if the Indians struck our camp, they would be sure to plunder it and we would be there without supplies of any kind. Fortunately, they missed our camp and went straight on their raid. That night, we hid our horses in a little deep creek near our camp. The next morning, we were off after our calf's hide and hams pretty early. As it was now near the full of the moon and we were certain the Indians were in, we started for home and all stayed with the wagon so as to be ready in the event we encountered a bunch of Indians.

There was a dim wagon road that led off in a northeast direction that we knew would lead us to settlements and, following this road until well into the evening, we were sure we saw an Indian ride off of a hill some distance to our right. This put us again on our guard and, as it began to get late in the evening, I was riding along just behind the wagon and saw, off to our left about a half mile, a bunch of ponies with their heads all turned in unison. I spoke to Brannin and Pool and told them to get their cartridges up in the wagon seat between them, for I knew well that there were a bunch of Indians lying in the grass where those ponies were.

We were ready in the event that they made an attack on us, but as we moved right on without any change in any way, the Indians made no move until we had gone far enough for a little rocky hill to come between us and them. I told the boys to turn off of the road and keep down a little swag that led on down to a brushy creek. This maneuver would keep the little hill between them and the Indians. I turned right up the side of the hill until I could see the Indians, who had gotten up from the grass and were mustering around as if they were fixing to charge us. But then they all came together in a little bunch for consultation.

As the road led on along the side of a long ridge and I knew that it crossed a deep brushy creek at the far end of this ridge, it was no surprise that the Indians struck out for that brushy creek, evidently intending to ambush us there. I at once galloped down the swag as our wagon had done until I overtook it on the main creek. I told the boys that I had counted twenty Indians on foot and ten on horseback. We all at once concluded that since they had ten to our one, we didn't want to fight them. So we didn't go back to the road, but continued our retreat down the creek until we found another road that would lead us to Jacksboro or Fort Richardson. There, we could report to the troops there that the Indians were on a raid. We had eluded those Indians and little runs such as this enabled me to retain my scalp until the Indian troubles were all over.

That night, as we moved down the creek, we came to a very dense thicket where the green briers were running all through the trees and brush. We stopped our wagon at the edge of this thicket and, as it now began to get a little dark, we trampled down a good spot in the thicket and put our horses in there. We made down our beds at the opening where we took the horses into the thicket so the Indians couldn't get to them without going over us. Tying our three watchful dogs out around our camp, we felt we were safe enough to get a good night's sleep.

The next morning, as we started on down the creek, we saw an Indian on top of a little hill off some distance from us. After standing there on his horse, he then galloped off in a northwesterly direction and soon disappeared from view. We didn't understand it at the time, but we met some men at Fort Richardson who told us that the Indians had been in and stolen all of the horses off of Doc Cooper's ranch. They were going right up the same way that we had been coming down and there were at least twenty of them. We knew then that the Indian we had seen in the morning was one of their spies, and that we had narrowly escaped meeting that raiding party. We were satisfied, too, that they were the same Indians that had come near our camp the evening before we left the buffalo range.

Since so many Indians were about and it was a full moon, and because we had been in such close quarters with them at several different places, I began to feel uneasy about my family at home. They were in a part of the country that was often visited by the Indians when they were in on a raid. So that night when we got into Jacksboro, I told the boys that I was going home the next day and they could now take their time and come on in with the meat.

The next morning when we arose, the ground was covered with six inches of snow. Pool and Brannin both told me that it would be a very hard, cold ride and that I would nearly freeze. I told them I planned to take that buffalo calf hide and would wrap my feet and legs in it. They both said that I would never get that green, bloody thing onto old brown Jim, since he was such a fool and so easily scared by anything of that kind. I said that if they would help me, I would work the calf hide onto him and, putting a strong pair of rawhide hopples on him then blindfolding him with a heavy handkerchief, they held him until I successfully worked the hide onto him.

I wrapped myself up good in a heavy overcoat and got on old brown Jim, then wrapped my feet and legs in the soft green calf's hide. Then I got one of the boys to take the hopples off and the other to jerk the blindfold off. Old Jim brought a loud snort and away he went down the road toward Decatur, in Wise County, which was nine miles from my home. The first half of the day, all I had to do to get him to go a little faster was to just shake one of my feet, which were still wrapped in the green calf hide. Jim would spring off at a lively gait until. By the evening, when the snow was very soft, old Jim got so tired that an Indian could hardly have scared him.

That day while I was on the road from Jacksboro to Decatur, I passed the trail of some Indians that I thought were going toward my home. Instead, though, they swung back more south and headed in a different direction, so I was not so uneasy anymore about home. When I reached Decatur, my horse was very tired and so was I. It was now about dark, so I went to the Grider House, the only hotel in Decatur at the time. Since I knew the people there well, I walked right into the hotel office with my buffalo calf hide in hand, as I wanted it kept where it wouldn't freeze.

When I got seated in the hotel dining room, I found there were quite a number of people there that I knew. Some of them from the country and others of the town all began at once asking me about the Indian news. This was most always the case when anyone came in from the west. I, of course, told them that the Indians were in pretty bad and that I was afraid that they were making a big raid under the big moon.

As I went on telling them the Indian news, I noticed they kept smiling and looking at each other, and I knew that some kind of joke was up. I also noticed that there was a well-dressed stranger sitting there, but he was quiet and kept perfect silence while the others were all talking. I paid little attention to him and, being very tired, I soon called for a bed and retired. The next morning when I got back among them, they told me I had run that fellow off. They said that the evening before, when he came in on the stage, he was loaded down with fine guns and plenty of ammunition. He said he was going to teach them all how to kill buffalo and that he would kill out the Indians who were stealing the horses. He thought it was very foolish for the people to sit there and not arm themselves up and kill out the Indians. But that night when he saw me come in off of the buffalo range and heard the report of actual Indians being in on a raid, he became alarmed and took the first stage out for the east. He was gone before I got out the next morning.

There are very few people that can go right out from a quiet peaceful country where they have always felt secure and go to where they have to face the dangers of a frontier life, and remain there satisfied. If they have some ties to bind them until they become accustomed to the wild country, they will then take hold of the excitements and become enamored by them. They become so inured to the life that they will stay and become permanent citizens. The establishment of a home to which settlers become attached and around which their every interest centers had more to do in settling this country than anything else.

Of course, there were quiet times when the Indians would not be in for a long while. During times like this, people would become so established in their homes that they would then stay and defend them to the death, especially if there was a family to be protected. I know that anyone who thinks of the Indians making a raid into the settlements would assume that every man who was not a base coward should seize his arms and be out after them in hot pursuit. But to those of us that have had experience along this line, it is very plain to see that the bravest and best of men would think first of protection of their homes and of the innocent and defenseless ones that were dependent upon them there. This was the main reason why I didn't join in to pursue and punish every band of Indians out of the many that raided through the country where I lived.

The Indians would often wait for a long while to let people get to feeling secure and to be off their guard. In this way, the Indians could do the greatest amount of damage. They would come pouring into the country often at two or three different points at once and no one ever knew just which way they were going. So every man that had a family thought first of having them protected. By the time this was done, the Indians had made their raids and were gone and there was no time for pursuit. To avoid pursuit after their raids, the Indians traveled day and night until they were way back into the wild, unsettled country again, not even stopping to secure food or sleep.

THE INDIANS' FOOD SUPPLY FOR RAIDS

This, to anyone not acquainted with the conditions that existed in those early days on the frontier, may be a little mysterious. To think of a strong force of men moving hundreds of miles across the land, barren of any kind of food that was produced by the labor of man, does seem strange now. It could not be done now. Before I close, I want to tell you just why they couldn't do it now and why they could do it back then.

Not only the food for the raiders must be considered, but one must also consider the vast numbers of women and children that were to be fed in their camps, as well as the unlimited supply of dogs that they kept. One must also think that they never planted any seeds nor tilled the soil nor met any of their obligations that God put upon the creatures of his hand. It not only seems strange, but also is clear proof of the fact that the Indians were not the real owners of this country.

In addressing how the Indians obtained food while they were plundering our frontier settlements, I also hope to correct the false impression that it was a crime for the white man to kill out the buffalo.

To present this matter so that everybody can properly understand it, it will be best to give the topography of the western range country which extends from the northern lakes to the Gulf of Mexico. Over this vast range, the innumerable herds of buffalo roamed and they were migratory in their nature to a great extent. They would drift south in the winter until they simply filled the whole country from the Rocky Mountains on the west to the settlements on the east. From this source, the Indians obtained the greater part of their supply of both food and clothing, as well as their bedding. About the only real labor that they ever did was to kill and dry their meat and to dress their hides. The latter was often left to their white captives, or slaves.

To read the accounts of the captivity of Mrs. Kellog, Mrs. Plummer, Mrs. Wilson, the Goacher family and every white woman that was a captive for any length of time, will touch the sympathies of even the hardest-hearted man in the world. Throughout the vast range country, the streams flowing out of the Rocky Mountains flow in an eastern or southeastern direction. As the buffalo would drift south, they would come down across these streams. The Indians would camp along these streams in order to gather their supplies from the buffalo, both as they were coming south in the fall and as they were drifting back the next spring.

Not only did they Indians get their food supply from this source at their camps, but they would also dry up quantities of this meat to be used while on their raids made on white settlements. As such, I have always thought that the killing of the buffalo was more to subdue the wild Indians than anything else. While it looked wasteful at the time, by this means thousands of lives were saved and the country was brought into the present peaceful condition that we now enjoy. Not only did the killing of the buffalo cut off the Indians' supplies, it also took the buffalo out of the way of the stock business and enabled the stockman to go out and occupy the range with domestic stock.

This use of the land by stockmen could not have been safely undertaken until the buffalo were killed out and stopped from drifting back over the country every fall. They drifted in such vast numbers that they not only destroyed the range, but they also drifted the other stock out of the country. About the time the buffalo were being killed out, it seems that a well-connected train of circumstances came around tending to the same great end: the subjugation of the Indians.

Following the Civil War, peace was now fully restored to the Union. Our people were now permitted to arm themselves again, which they did in a proper way. In doing so, they were prepared with long-range guns with which they could kill the buffalo rapidly. Although it was done for the profit that existed in their hides and meat, the settlers could also use their fine guns on the Indians whenever they got a chance. The result was that there was at once a strong, self-supporting army put all along our frontier.

The Indians soon lived in mortal dread of buffalo hunters. They could see their meat supply being destroyed from Wyoming all down through Colorado, Kansas and Texas. I have counted on many occasions while I was killing buffalo as many as one hundred freshly killed and skinned buffalo frames. You see, when the experienced hunter with his long-range gun could kill the leader of the herd, the other buffalo would gather about him and stamp around until they were nearly all killed, or at least as many of them as the hunter desired. The man who did the killing was then followed by a force of men who did the skinning. The hunter did his killing in specific ways to suit the skinners.

About the time that all of this was going on, the United States government put forth her strong arm for the protection of the settlers and the subduing of the Indians. This was soon done and the government took a peaceful course with them, deciding it was easier to feed than to fight them. Since all of these circumstances seemed to combine in bringing the desired result, we can now justify the course pursued on the grounds that we are a Christian nation, living out the principles that Christ taught: "If thine enemy hunger, feed them; if he thirst, give him drink."

And now, by kindness, we ought to get hold of their affections and confidence. I am glad to say that there has been a wonderful change sweeping across the Indians in the last few years. Many of them are becoming Christians. Some of them are now preachers of the gospel and are going as missionaries among their own people, and all of the Indians are in a far better condition than they were while in a wild state. They no longer seek their support from wild game, nor do they have to plunder and steal for a livelihood. Instead, they have a living furnished for them for free, a moderate supply of clothing for free and very good educational advantages for free, and all at a cost to our government that can hardly be noticed.